Unraveling the Seven Riddles of the Universe

D0613396

Unraveling the Seven Riddles of the Universe

Alexander R. Mazziotti

HAMILTON BOOKS
an imprint of

ROWMAN & LITTLEFIELD
Lanham • Boulder • New York • London

Published by Hamilton Books
An imprint of The Rowman & Littlefield Publishing Group, Inc.
4501 Forbes Boulevard, Suite 200, Lanham, Maryland 20706
www.rowman.com

86-90 Paul Street, London EC2A 4NE, United Kingdom

British Library Cataloguing in Publication Information Available

Library of Congress Cataloging-in-Publication Data Available

ISBN 9780761872894 (pbk : alk. paper) | ISBN 9780761872900 (ebook)

∞™ The paper used in this publication meets the minimum requirements of American National Standard for Information Sciences—Permanence of Paper for Printed Library Materials, ANSI/NISO Z39.48-1992.

Contents

Preface

A riddle generally has a veiled meaning almost like a parable. The challenge of a riddle can be intriguing. This book is about seven fundamental riddles that our universe presents us with. The origin of the presentation of these riddles goes back to a speech given on August 14, 1872 by Emil Du Bois-Reymond, a famous physiologist, entitled "The Limits of Natural Science" and addressed to the Scientific Congress at Leipzig, Germany. Emil had applied science to understand how electricity flows in our nerves and muscles, which at the time resulted in a great blow to those who believed in Vitalism. He presented these seven riddles with the belief that some of them would probably never be solved. This speech marked the beginning of the end of the existing scientific euphoria regarding the notion that we, through science, could understand everything. With the coming turn of the century, Einstein founded the theory of relativity and then de Broglie, Schrodinger, Bohr, Heisenberg, and others ushered in the quantum world of uncertainty.

The idea for this book originated from finding an old book: Haeckel, Ernst. *The Riddle Of The Universe At The Close Of The Nineteenth Century* (Harper Brothers, 1905). Haeckel's view, in contrast to Emil's, was that most of the seven riddles were solved or solvable. Upon reading the book, I wanted to find out how one might currently view the riddles, who Emil Du Bois-Reymond was, and what led him to speak about the riddles. I was intrigued by the book in that it was written at a time just before the world of physics was about to undergo a revolution. The seven riddles are:

1. The Ultimate Nature of Matter, Energy, and Force
2. The Origin of Motion
3. The Origin of Life
4. Is there a Pre-Ordained Purpose (Teleology) for Living Beings?

5. The Origin of Sensations
6. The Origin of Consciousness, Language, and Rational Thought
7. Does man have Free Will?

   In this book, we examine each of the seven riddles in relation to current knowledge. Chapter one describes the life and times of Emil Du Bois-Reymond, a man who possessed a tremendous intellect, a vivid imagination, and who found great joy in science and truth. The riddles converge on riddle number four, which is the question regarding the ultimate purpose of our lives. The riddles nest together science and philosophy as we emphasize a global picture based on Alfred North Whitehead's Process Philosophy. Beyond philosophy, we discuss the role of faith versus nihilism in interpreting the incomplete riddles since the human journey is a continual struggle between reason and faith. We also examine what are called 'second tier riddles' which encompass mankind's moral problems such as the elimination of violence and discuss their essential connections to the global riddles.

   Current U.S. religious institutions are in serious trouble as many young adults, now about fifty percent, view them as irrelevant and do not plan to raise their children in them. In addition to their concern about the rise of violent religious extremism, they believe that people who subscribe to organized religion are often more intolerant of differing opinions. They perceive religious leaders as weak moral examples often espousing political agendas that hurt the poor, the disenfranchised, and immigrants.

   Part two responds to our conclusions on the need for a deity by examining two theologies which are consistent with the process approach, namely in alignment with fundamental human needs and are a sound attempt at making sense of the remaining unknowns within the seven riddles. In addition to a further examination of Process Theology we consider Social Theology which was developed by the teacher and scholar William DeWitt Hyde. A chapter will also discuss DeWitt Hyde's life and other works. Religion's future trajectory and its relationship to science are investigated. The notion of the miraculous and the possibility of an afterlife are probed. All our endeavors ultimately can yield for us some wisdom in our lives. The nature of wisdom is surveyed.

   We believe that those in organized religions and those outside of them can learn from this analysis and that appropriate religious strength and religious institutions are still very important for a society currently plagued by unacceptable school, church, mall, etc. shootings and declining life expectancy from both drug dependency and Covid-19.

   The nearly 150 years since Du Bois-Reymond's speech have seen remarkable advances in science and medicine, but each generation confronts, consciously or not, the riddles of the universe using their entire set of family and religious beliefs, their current knowledge, experience, and emotion to formulate internally a faith for themselves as life evolves. We hope this book helps you to find value and purpose for yourself, your family, and those you encounter during your life's journey. We also hope it results in your appreciation of the tremendous contributions that science has made to society, especially at this time when science and reason have often been brutalized by political whim.

I wish to thank my sons, David and Mark, for their unfailing support and for their reading of the manuscript. A special thanks to my wife, Janet, whose love and timeless encouragement has made this book possible. Also, I would like to express my appreciation to the countless scientific researchers and philosophers who have vastly extended our knowledge of the riddles since the time of Du Bois-Reymond. Finally, to my parents who steadfastly retained and shared their faith in God, family, and humanity through good and difficult times.

Alexander Mazziotti M.D., Ph.D.
Hawthorne, New Jersey
June, 2021

Part I

UNRAVELING THE SEVEN RIDDLES OF THE UNIVERSE

Chapter 1

Emil Du Bois-Reymond

The Man and his Work

Who was the man who postulated the seven riddles of the universe and understood the limitations of science despite the tremendous progress of the scientific research of his time? Emil Du Bois-Reymond was born on November 7, 1818, in Berlin. His father, Felix-Henri was from French controlled Neuchatel where he had been a teacher and moved to Berlin in 1804 with his wife, Minette Henry, a Huguenot. Neuchatel had just come under the control of the King of Prussia and the move was facilitated by the fact that Minette's father was a French diplomat in Berlin. In Berlin, Felix was a civil servant and a diplomat, but Felix remained a teacher and researcher at heart. However, both of his sons became successful in academic careers.

Emil was one of five children and in his youth, his parents believed he was inferior to his brother, Gustavo. At six years old, Gustavo unfortunately died of scarlet fever, and his father never fully recovered from the tremendous loss. Emil's younger brother, Paul, was born when Emil was thirteen and ultimately became a famous mathematician. Paul was aided by his older brother in his development. Interestingly, Paul's work on partial differential equations led to the realization that limitations existed in understanding fundamental mathematical foundations. He highlighted a particular continuous function that could be nowhere differentiable, seemingly contradicting mathematical intuition. He wrote at the time, "I cannot help thinking that entering deeper into the matter will finally lead us to the limits of our intellect."[1] Thus, he shared with his brother his belief in the grandeur and the limitations of scientific and mathematical endeavors.

During his youth, Emil enjoyed family trips, and he kept detailed diaries of them. He particularly liked the visit to his dad's hometown in France and frolicked in the forest with new friends. He would later spend a year at school near the area. In 1836, he entered the University of Berlin and eventually transferred to the University of Bonn. He was initially interested in history and philosophy but then he dabbled in geology. However, he eventually fell in love with medicine and physiology. Emil was athletic and enjoyed swimming, hiking, and horseback riding.

He was fortunate enough to have Johannes Muller, a famous physiology professor, take him under his wing. Muller was a vitalist because he believed that physical laws could only explain living beings to a certain extent, and he felt that science should attempt to apply these laws as much as possible with careful observation and experimentation. In that framework, he gave Emil a copy of a paper concerning the electric properties of animals written by the Italian researcher, Carlo Matteucci. Emil loved the topic yet he found that some of Matteucci's work while groundbreaking was often not carefully conducted.

Emil improved the methods of study and created new instruments to better verify and quantify the results. In 1841, Emil confirmed with the use of a galvanometer that an electrical impulse in a frog's nerve was responsible for the frog's movement. He published his work without the full details to avoid giving Matteucci any, in his opinion, unfair advantage. He understood that chemicals in the body were somehow responsible for nerve transmission, and he even alluded to the notion of what would eventually be discovered and called the synapse. In 1848, he showed that current flowed from the back to the front of the eye when the eye was illuminated.

The year 1848 was also a time of revolution in Germany. As was happening in other European monarchies, there was a demand for a representative government. On March 10, workers rioted in Berlin. Emil wrote to his life-long friend and fellow scientist, Carl Ludwig, about this and said,

"It is the great, new, glorious era that has befallen us." Also, "This endless night continued thus until five in the morning, when, within my hearing range, the battle ceased. After a few hours' sleep, all Berlin went out into its streets, for the most part to see what had actually been going on. The description I give you here does in fact fit the great majority of all people of our stamp. What a site the streets were! covered with scattered barricades, with tiles smashed from the roofs, the pavement torn up, the windows and walls shot to pieces, front doors smashed in, and, here and there, blood! Dying people were borne on stretchers, respectfully the crowd made way, gazing with bared heads after the almost envied sufferers, an ominous, portentous determination in all eyes, in all fists, as they now appeared. Now everyone knew what had happened; now everyone was ready to let his blood flow for liberty...."[2]

In a short time, King William of Prussia agreed to some of the demands of the opposition and set up a Parliament; however, over a period of months, he slowly undermined the changes and by the first day of April, the Parliament was dissolved, and the "revolution" was over.

Returning his focus to science, in 1849 Emil measured current flow in a muscle as it contracted. His work was met with considerable disbelief and resistance at the time.

He was friends with Hermann von Helmholtz and Rudolf Clausius, both of whom helped to lay the foundations of thermodynamics, and are well known to today's students of physics and chemistry. By 1850, his work was slowing and he lived alone in a small apartment, and he was losing faith in science because of his critics and his inability to obtain a professorship.

In 1852, he traveled to England and there he met a distant cousin named Jeannette Claude whom he courted and married. The wedding, which was held on August 22, 1853, was an English country wedding in Ambleside, which is a lake area in northwest England. Ambleside is a beautiful area even today and a great travel spot. After the wedding, they spent a fortnight at Henry Bence-Jones' vacant house in West London. Bence-Jones, a physician and a chemist, is well known for discovering Bence-Jones proteins, which can occur with myeloma. From there, they went to Folkestone district near the English Channel, where Bence-Jones had his seaside home. Carl Ludwig, on hearing the news of the marriage, wrote to him wisely: "Follow the advice of the experienced married man and give yourself over entirely to the first years of matrimony; one is never as happy before and will never be as happy again after, not because love wanes, but because the host of worries about children and so forth does not fail to appear and does not allow the idle, serene, epicurean relish of the first years to arise later." Emil wrote to Ludwig, "Marriage has made me young again, i.e., life once again lies spread out before me apparently without limit; if only money, too, were never-ending, aside from time and space."[3]

Jeannette returned to Berlin with him and his fortunes improved. In 1851, he had been elected to the Prussian Academy of Sciences. In 1855, he was appointed associate professor at the University of Berlin and in the same year, a son, Claude, was born. By 1858, he had become full professor of physiology after the passing of his beloved mentor, Johannes Muller. In 1866, he became the Dean of the Medical School.

His work occurred well before the discovery of the electron and paved the way for common tests used today such as the EKG, EEG, and EMG and, with the eventual characterization of the positively charged proton and the positron, to MRI and PET scans. In his later years, Emil became interested in social and philosophical issues, as he had been in his youth. In 1870, he gave a speech widely covered in the press that dealt in part with Carl Menger's (the economist) criticism of pragmatic interpretations of social institutions. On August 14, 1872, he gave his famous speech on the absolute limits of our knowledge about the world and the seven mysteries, which we will re-examine in the following chapters. It was ironic that the man who killed vitalism also killed science as a god and knowledge as unbounded. He wrote to Carl Ludwig two weeks after the speech,

"Have you read the reporter's review of my speech in the national paper? He praises it highly but criticizes it for not having been extemporaneous. That's what I call a bit too much, expecting one to get up before 2,000 people and speak for three-quarters of an hour on the limits of physics and metaphysics without any preparation. By the way, he did not even get the point."[4]

Emil clearly saw that the press definitely had its limits regarding knowledgeable reporting. In Emil's last letter to Ludwig dated September 28, 1894, he stated,

"I spent the vacation on the Mediterranean, in a little nest behind Genoa, where every day I plunged into the depths from the boat with my wife and was occasionally cast onto the rocks by the waves, like Odysseus. If one can still do that 23 times in 28 days when one is going on 76, then one must be satisfied with one's neuromuscular system and can count on being fit for work for a couple more years."[5]

Ludwig responded on October 4, 1894,

"I was pleased, therefore, to hear that you feel strong and that you enjoy being active. I also hear often and gladly that your two elder sons are living in distinguished and lucrative circumstances that the younger one is busy studying chemistry, and, what is no less gratifying, that your daughters are winning recognition and other gratification as an artist and a writer. And finally, as I see that you are always mentally alert and active, I know you have a happy old age and will continue to enjoy that happiness for a long while yet, for the good of the academy and of your students."[6]

Unfortunately, Emil Du Bois-Reymond passed away a little over a couple of years later on December 26, 1896.[7]

NOTES

1. O'Connor, JJ and Robertson EF, *Paul DuBois-Reymond*, 2005.
2. DuBois-Reymond, Estelle, *Two Great Scientists*, 1982, 10.
3. DuBois-Reymond, Estelle, 1982, 82.

4. DuBois-Reymond, Estelle, 1982, 112.
5. DuBois-Reymond, Estelle, 1982, 120.
6. DuBois-Reymond, Estelle, 1982, 121.
7. Finkelstein, Gabriel. *Emil du Bois-Reymond*, 2013.

Chapter 2

Riddle 1

Ultimate Nature of Matter, Force, and Energy

INANIMATE MATTER AND ENERGY— QUANTUM THEORY AND RELATIVITY

At the time of Du Bois-Reymond's speech at the end of the nineteenth century, the ultimate nature of matter and energy was viewed from a different perspective than today. The general feeling was that physics had progressed as much as possible because Newtonian physics along with Maxwell's equations for light and radiation could theoretically describe our material world fully. Emil rightly believed that the ultimate nature of matter and energy was probably much more complex than what was already known.

Newton's laws of motion were well established as well as the mathematical description of the laws based on calculus. It seemed as if one could theoretically predict the future when working with Newton's equations. In the 1800s, James Clerk Maxwell developed a theory of electricity and magnetism. Thus, at the end of the nineteenth century one had two theories that seemed to explain matter and energy; however, that was about to change.

Physicists were confident about these theories, but a number of anomalies arose that needed to be resolved; however, the resolution of these anomalies would turn the scientific world upside down. One of these anomalies was blackbody radiation, which is a measurement of radiation emanating from a thermodynamically stable closed box with just a pinhole in it. It turned out that the existing theories could not fully describe the system over varying temperatures and conditions. The problem was solved in 1901 by Max Planck who saw that it was necessary to have quantized or packets in the energy of the radiation rather than a continuous spectrum. In 1905, Einstein, using Planck's insight of radiation having packets, characterized the photoelectric effect. This effect occurs when one shines a light on a metal and observes the electrons that are kicked off the metal. He found that one could account for the experimental results only if the light energy was quantized. Therefore, radiation came in packets, not just waves, and as a result, quantum theory emerged.[1]

Around the same time the electron and proton were being characterized, a model for the hydrogen atom was postulated. A larger +1 charged proton in the center and a smaller electron, -1 charged, orbited around the proton. By allowing the orbits to have quantized energy rather than being continuous, Niels Bohr created a model that accounted for the radiation emitted by the atom after excitation and relaxation known as the spectrum of the atom. The nature of the spectral lines seen in experiments corresponded to the transition between the quantized energy levels. However, one problem existed with the theory; the quantization was an add-on rather than fitting into the rest of classical physics.

Louis de Broglie, a young graduate student in France, was then pursuing his doctorate in physics, and he postulated in his thesis that, as Einstein had shown that light could have wave properties and particle properties, matter could have wave properties as well as the obvious matter properties. His thesis committee did not want to award him his thesis because the concept seemed so outlandish. It just so happened that Einstein was visiting the university at the time of his thesis presentation, and the doctoral committee asked him whether he should be awarded his thesis, and Einstein said that yes, he thought he should, and that the result was potentially a major achievement. In 1929 after the wave properties were experimentally verified, Louis de Broglie was awarded the Nobel Prize in physics. This discovery led Erwin Schrödinger in 1925 to derive the fundamental quantum mechanical equation named after him. This equation solved the problem with the Bohr atomic theory and set the stage for the battle about the implication and meaning of the wave function.

Werner Heisenberg in 1925 developed a similar complementary approach to quantum computation using matrices. Then, in 1927, he introduced the Quantum Uncertainty Principle which proved that because of the wave properties of matter, quantum theory was limited in terms of the information obtainable at a given time for a given system. With a classical particle such as a baseball, you can find both the position and the momentum of the particle, as it moves. In contrast, a quantum particle has limitations. For example, if you obtain the position of the particle exactly, then you lose all of the information about the momentum and vice versa. If you know a little bit about the position within some bound, then the Heisenberg Uncertainty Equation tells you how uncertain the momentum will be. When a very small particle such as an electron is hit with a light wave in order to measure its position, you transfer momentum to the particle so that while you're finding out the position of the particle, you disturb the momentum and vice versa.

In 1926, Max Born, a German scientist, showed that the probability of finding a particle at a given position for a quantum system was related to the square of the wave function, which emerged from the calculations. For all of the other variables, such as energy and momentum, they were also proportional to the square of the wave function. Now, the classical picture of the nineteenth century in which Du Bois lived is gone, and our ability to track the reality of small particles is lost and has been replaced by probabilities. This does not mean that we can't use the quantum equations and garnish a lot of information about matter, but there are inherent limitations as to what we can know.

Statistical mechanics encompassed entropy along with quantum theory and allowed the interpretation of energy transfer in systems with large numbers of particles. Einstein, who contributed to the development of quantum mechanics through the analysis of the photoelectric effect, revolutionized the notions of space and time with the development of relativity theory. Space and time were no longer independent of one another. Time could contract or expand, and space could bend. This was possible because Einstein realized the result of the Michelson-Morley experiment, which showed that the speed of light was unchanging to any observer, could only be understood in his relativity framework. The work on relativity also led to his famous equation, $E=mc^2$, which shows that matter and energy are interchangeable. As a particle gives up energy, a small amount of matter is lost. In this concept, the awful possibility of releasing tremendous amounts of energy stored in the nucleus of the atom emerged and with it the dread of nuclear weapons.

BIOLOGIC SYSTEMS—ENTROPY AND COMPLEXITY

Now let's look at biophysical energy, matter, and force. In the biological realm, Du Bois-Reymond would be amazed to see the progress that has been made since his lifetime. As complex as the physical and chemical matter is, biological matter has chemical systems in a complex coordination with the aim of preservation of a self-sustaining and reproducible entity. In order to understand physical, biological, and biochemical systems, one has to understand the physical chemical concept of entropy, which is essential to understand biochemical change.

Entropy is intimately related to the process of change. Most things are not easily reversible so the tendency toward disorder is a fundamental aspect of our world. If one opens up a slot between two gas containers with different non-interacting molecules on each side at the same temperature and pressure, they're going to mix and become more disordered, which increases the entropy of this system. It takes energy to keep order in a biologic system and overcome the entropic forces of decay or dissolution. As mentioned previously, Du Bois-Reymond realized that the same principles that control inanimate physical systems should be able to explain most biologic processes. His teacher, German physician-physiologist Johannes Peter Muller, once wrote in his book *Elements of Physiology:* "Though there appears to be something in the phenomena of living beings which cannot be explained by ordinary mechanical, physical or chemical laws, much may be so explained, and we may without fear push these explanations as far as we can, so long as we keep to the solid ground of observation and experiment."[2]

Biologic systems are made up of a huge number of chemical reactions, each of which is often near equilibrium to keep a steady state. As an example of the complexity, let us look at the single cell organism, Mycoplasma genitalium, which can cause a sexually transmitted disease in humans. It has only 525 genes, one of the smallest for a single cell organism. Recently, a research group from Stanford attempted to model the cell on a computer.[3] It actually took 128 computers running for hours just to generate the data on the twenty-five categories of molecules that are involved in the cell's processes. The M. genitalium model required twenty-eight subsystems, including DNA and RNA activities, protein management, and energy and chromosome production to be detailed and integrated together. Even with this accomplishment, the model is primitive and limited. However, unlike in the 1800s, we have an understanding of DNA replication and instructions with RNA directed protein production, etc. The biologic activities of simple cells are consistent with the modern laws of chemistry and physics that deal with energy and entropy, but they are not fully grasped by a chemistry and physics reductionist analysis. This is even more so as we delve into the complexity of a human being.

HUMAN MIND, INFORMATION, AND SPIRITUAL ENERGY

Evolving from a single cell organism to the human mind is an unbelievable leap in terms of the complexity of the material world that is needed to create human consciousness and emotion, rational thought, and creativity. Directed energy rather than entropy is representative of purposeful information. While the laws of physics and chemistry are active in the major entanglement of trillions of neurons, the exact mechanism is not known, and some have speculated that the entanglement from quantum mechanics may be at the heart of the development of consciousness.[4] We are conscious beings just like other animals; however, our rational nature and self-analysis significantly surpasses the other members of the animal kingdom.

Information can be thought of as the resolution of uncertainty. For example, if I pick and have a number between one and n in mind, then for the case of n=100, one has more information entropy than n=2. More work is usually involved in the first case than in the second in assessing and determining that number. If there are only two choices and I tell you that the number you chose is wrong, then you know what the other number is. In the former example, if I tell you that your guess of fifty is wrong, then you still do not know the answer since there are ninety-nine possibilities remaining. Acquiring knowledge often requires trial and error, and complicated problems require more attempts in order to solve them. The human brain has approximately ten billion neurons. Although the average adult human brain weighs only about two percent of our total body weight, it demands around twenty percent of our resting metabolic energy.

The energy of the human spirit is based on external information as well as self-information and self-identity. The spirit and the body are symbiotic; each feeds the other. The human spirit carries the cross between the self and others. This spiritual energy cannot be described solely in physical terms because information, logic, and emotion deal with abstractions. The human mind must make value judgments. Why are we here and how should I live my life? Whom do I trust and whom do I love? Concepts of justice, love, law, peace, deity, and dignity tend to emerge as answers to these questions. Value judgments are complex, and it is difficult to predict the course of human decisions. While he believed in evolution, Du Bois did not believe that science would fully explain the nature of human consciousness. As has been previously stated, in the realm of inanimate and biologic matter, we now have a truly amazing understanding of the forces and energy that control them; however, we can't say our comprehension is complete. Even more importantly, when it comes to human spiritual energy, we confront abstract notions that are not completely applicable to a reductionist approach of physical science. Not only are matter and energy interchangeable but energy and information are also interchangeable. Similarly, with information comes being and with being comes the power of the individual and society. While the latter are a function of the variables, matter and energy, they are also only understandable by introducing additional abstract variables. Therefore, matter, energy, and spirit are complex, and we will further discuss this in future chapters.

NOTES

1. Gamow, George, *Thirty Years that Shook Physics*, 2012.
2. Muller, Johannes, *Elements of Physiology*, 1838, 1–918.
3. McClure, Max, *Mycoplasma*, July 2012.
4. Penrose, Roger, *Shadows of the Mind*, 1994.

Chapter 3

Riddle 2

The Origin of Motion

The world we have inherited is one of continual change, and this would not be possible if there were not ordering laws imposed on matter and the fact that distinguishable entities exist. Du Bois-Reymond was concerned about whether we could ever know the origin of such motion in our universe. In the late 1800s, many scientists viewed the universe as infinite in time and space. Matter exists, and it is always in motion and always will. The other view of the universe as a wound-up clock slowly losing energy was enforced by the new concept of entropy and as an origin of creation; it was somewhat consistent with biblical creation.

It was difficult to imagine then that one could ever scientifically trace back what happened so long ago, but today we have strong evidence to support a theory known as the Big Bang. Yet even with that understanding, we always return to the same philosophical questions such as what caused the Big Bang or why did it occur. We will start this discussion with the science behind the Big Bang.

SCIENCE FROM THE LATE 1800s TO THE PRESENT

Notions about the origins of motion go back to the beginning of human history. With Isaac Newton a quantitative understanding developed. Newtonian mechanics alone had allowed for an understanding of most planetary motions around the Sun, but it was only with Einstein's relativistic equations that a mathematical description of what was happening in the whole universe was conceived. Furthermore, at the turn of the twentieth century, the field of astronomy was rapidly advancing. The first recognition from spectroscopy of receding galaxies was noted through a redshift (towards lower frequencies) in the spectral lines of emitted light.

In 1915, Einstein published his theory of general relativity and in 1917, he used the equation to model the universe. While doing so, he had a conundrum in that with a certain constant added he believed he could keep the universe static. He would later say this was the biggest mistake of his career although it later became useful in explaining the expanding universe. Alexander Friedmann, a Russian professor, who fought as an army aviator in World War I, applied Einstein's relativistic equations to the universe in 1922, and showed that three possibilities existed—an expanding, contracting, or a static universe. This would make the Big Bang model, the Steady State Model, and the Static Model possible. One of Friedmann's doctoral students was George Gamow who would make many contributions to physics and was the author of a popular book called: *One Two Three Infinity*, which brought scientific excitement to a generation of young people, including myself.[1]

Georges Lemaitre was a Belgian Roman Catholic Jesuit priest, an astronomer, and a professor of physics who had trained at Cambridge University and spent a year at Harvard University under the tutelage of Harlow Shapley, a famous American astronomer. On returning to Belgium to a teaching position in 1925, he independently used Einstein's equation in a form without the cosmological constant and proposed an expanding universe. Reasoning backward in time, he concluded that the universe expanded from a small size, which later became known as the Big Bang theory. On reading his paper, Einstein said, "Your calculations are correct, but your physics is atrocious."[2] A few years later, the astronomer, Hubble, had data showing the expanding universe, and the constant of expansion, later known as the Hubble constant, which had first been predicted by Lemaitre.

Soon after Einstein's original relativistic work, another German physicist astronomer solved Einstein's equations for a massive rotating disk. He accomplished this while serving in the army during World War I. The disk model predicted the event horizon at the edge of what eventually would be found and known as a black hole. Unfortunately, he died from an autoimmune illness, which developed while he was on the Russian front lines. His name was Karl Schwarzschild.

What makes us believe that the Big Bang hypothesis is true besides the expanding universe verified by astronomers? Einstein's special and general relativity theories have been proven repeatedly to describe reality accurately. The first test was the abnormal motion in Mercury's orbit that could not be understood by Newtonian mechanics. Einstein's theory explained it completely because the Sun in close proximity to Mercury warped the nearby space, and this resolved the kinky orbit. The warping of light around a massive body known as gravitational lensing was predicted by general relativity. Observations of the lensing of stars near the Sun during eclipses in 1919 and 1922 further confirmed his theory and led to Einstein's receipt of the Nobel Prize. The nearby stars would normally not be visible but with a total solar eclipse, the light and light bending could be and was measured. Such lensing has since helped find planets around distant stars because the planets act as a perturbation on the bending.

Black holes, which were predicted in 1915 as mentioned above, were first indirectly detected in 1971 by the astronomer, Tom Bolton, from the observation of X-ray binary stars. While the recent detection of gravitational waves from collisions of ancient black holes (LIGO project) is known through geographically separated detectors, it is also utilized by the relativity equations that predicted their existence. The data analysis has given significant information about the nature of the black holes that were not previously available.

Finally, the development of GPS satellites critically depend upon both special and general relativity equations to take into account the time difference between Earth and the satellites. Thus, since 1918, the equations have been tested and shown to work repeatedly. Next, we will analyze further evidence for the Big Bang theory itself.

How sure are we of The Big Bang?

In addition to the evidence of a strong, expanding universe that is consistent with relativity theory already presented above, other more recent evidence involves the following:

1. Cosmic Background Radiation

The Big Bang theory predicts that the universe was initially very, very hot. This can be understood because reversibly the universe when contracted would absorb tremendous amounts of energy. Physicists reasoned we should now be able to find some remnant of this enormous heat. In 1965, Radio astronomers Arno Penzias and Robert Wilson of Bell Labs discovered a 2.725 degree Kelvin (-454.765 degree Fahrenheit) microwave background radiation that pervades the sky. Robert Dicke of Princeton University who had studied the notion of the Big Bang recognized that the results of the Penzias and Wilson experiment were consistent with the leftover radiation from the Big Bang. Together they published the paper with mostly an emphasis on the experimental facts. Penzias and Wilson shared in the 1978 Nobel Prize for physics for their discovery. More developments on the Cosmic Background Radiation hypothesis will be given below.[3]

2. *Abundance of Light Elements in the Universe*

The abundance of the "light elements," Hydrogen and Helium, found in the observable universe are thought to support the Big Bang model of origins. With the knowledge of what is known as The Standard Model of fundamental particles, developed in the 1970s, scientists categorized known particles and ultimately predicted the existence of new particles, which were eventually found, culminating with the Higgs boson in 2012. With this knowledge, the expectation of the appearance of different particles in the various stages of the early universe could be elucidated. The ratios of the known different isotopes of Hydrogen are consistent with what is postulated for the early universe in the Big Bang theory. This is also true for other light elements.

3. COBE Satellite Data

In 1989, NASA launched the [Cosmic Background Explorer satellite] (COBE), for a more detailed analysis of the microwave background radiation, which emanates from the first formation of neutral atoms, namely Hydrogen, and an expected temperature of about 3,000 K.

In 1990, high-precision spectrum measurements showed that the cosmic microwave background (CMB) frequency spectrum is an almost perfect blackbody (absorbs and emits all frequencies and has a characteristic curve for a given temperature) with no deviations at a level of one part in 104, and measured a residual temperature of 2.726 K. This temperature and this degree of cooling are consistent with the expansion of the universe as would be expected at the time of the Big Bang.

In 1992, further COBE measurements discovered tiny fluctuations (anisotropies) in the CMB temperature across the sky at a level of about one part in 105. The theory can account for these fluctuations due to factors such as radiation matter interactions in different regions of expansion space when one also takes into account the notions of dark matter and dark energy, which will be discussed.

4. *An Almost Flat Universe*

The CMB anisotropies were consistent with an almost flat shape of the universe. If it were curved, then the normal triangular measurements of points in space would be inaccurate. This flat universe is also consistent with physical observations of the night sky.

5. *Dark Energy and Dark Matter*

Besides fitting in with the COBE data, what evidence do we have for dark matter and dark energy? If we look at different galaxies and ours, we can estimate the mass of the stars involved in a particular galaxy and the rotation speed of that galaxy. The faster the stars rotate about the galactic center the more mass there must be to keep the stars bound, which can be seen by equating the centripetal force experienced by an orbiting star of a given mass with the gravitational force. When this is done, one realizes that some matter is missing, known as dark matter since it is not visible matter, and the particles involved are still not known.

More recently, measurements of the redshifts of supernovae indicate the expansion of the universe is accelerating, which is an observation attributed to dark energy's existence. The leading alternative theory for dark energy envisions it as a field that pervades space, similar to the "inflation field" that most cosmologists think drove the explosive inflation of the universe during the Big Bang. The gravity of dark matter makes the universe clumpier, but dark energy makes it less clumpy because it moves galaxies away from each other. We will discuss Inflation theory below.

The CMB mentioned previously used both factors to fit the existing data. Recently, the Dark Energy Survey (DES) looked at a smaller region of the sky with the hope of increasing the accuracy of the Hubble expansion rate, which now has slightly different values from the supernova redshift and CMB. Work on this resolution is occurring through the gravitational wave experiments—LIGO. Based on LIGO's increasing sensitivity and the assumed rate of neutron star mergers, scientists now expect to have enough data to decide between the two Hubble constant contenders within a few years.

6. Inflation

Inflation theory states that the universe expanded very early on at greater than the speed of light. The inflationary period stretched from ten to the minus thirty-six (power) seconds after the conjectured Big Bang singularity to sometime between ten to the minus thirty-three to ten to the minus thirty-two seconds after the singularity. Space actually stretched out comparatively from the size of a proton to that of a grapefruit. The distance between objects increased in proportion. Following the inflationary period, the universe continues to expand but at a less rapid rate.

The CMB has almost the exact same temperature in all directions. The argument is if you trace back the origin of the background radiation without inflation, then you find that the radiation that reached us from different directions was never in causal contact with each other. Why then does it have the same temperature in all directions? This problem, which inflation can solve, is known as the horizon problem. Inflation theory also helps explain the flatness problem, which was mentioned above, and the monopole problem, which arises from applying other aspects of theoretical physics to the cosmic evolution. Overall inflation theory is the weakest link in terms of support for the theory based on known fundamental physics.

Origin of Motion, Science, and the Deity

Science is based on knowledge of how matter and energy interact. Science assumes causality exists and is looking for causes that fit in with already accepted precepts. Studying how an apple fell from a tree and how other objects fall led to Newtonian mechanics as a general theory. Causality in science deals with some form of physical observation, but science cannot transcend matter and energy. Today's science should recognize the distinct spiritual energy of living material beings as an outcome of physical matter and energy even though it cannot recognize spiritual forces without incorporating matter or energy. Thus, to postulate that God, a purely spiritual being, created the world from nothing at the time of the Big Bang, is not in the realm of science. This does not mean that it could not be true. While Du Bois-Reymond believed in this notion of a creator, our science and our logic are unable to explain this concept.

If we assume the Big Bang came into existence from another universe, science is unable to explain why this is the case, and it is unclear why there are laws or why these particular laws and its corresponding order actually exists. If on the other hand, God is the spirit infusing the evolving universe, one contingent upon matter and energy, which is a pantheistic view, then the questions of the origin of motion from a purely spiritual being are muted. Therefore, all matter and energy has a spiritual pole guiding it. If this were so, then one would expect that besides the physical laws, spiritual laws would be manifest by revealing purpose and values, and teleology would appear to be a manifestation of God's presence and purpose. The physical beauty of the world would also be reflected through his presence. This resulting kind of spiritual world, regardless of the notion of pantheism or not, is the kind that we as humans have in general inherited through our ancestors who overall had very strong religious inclinations. This concept of God and purpose will be explored in depth in future chapters.

NOTES

1. Gamow, George, *One, Two, Three Infinity*, 1962.
2. Pomeroy, Ross, *Einstein*, 2017.
3. NASA, COBE, 2016.

Chapter 4

Riddle 3

The Origin of Life

What is life? The 1944 book by Erwin Schrodinger, the creator of the fundamental quantum equation that is named after him, has a title that asks the above question: *What is Life?* Schrodinger speculated on the notion of a key genetic molecule that would carry encoded information for life. After their discovery of DNA, Watson and Crick credited Schrodinger's book as one of their inspirations.[1]

It was around 1860 that Mendel, an Augustinian friar, ran his famous genetic experiments on pea plants. At that time, Du Bois firmly believed in the importance of some physical chemical mechanisms of life processes, and that he did not want to invoke Vitalism as the cause. Vitalism, a theory mostly accepted at the time, is the belief that living organisms are fundamentally different from non-living entities because they contain some non-physical aspects, and are governed by different principles than are inanimate things. Du Bois-Reymond would have been gratified by the discovery of DNA and the understanding about how DNA and RNA give instructions for protein production, etc. He would also be pleased that we now understand the numerous chemical pathways for energy transfer and production, the nature of the cell wall and/or cell membrane construction, and the role of epigenetics in genetic function and transmission.

Besides rapidly elucidating the genetic code for humans, recent advances in gene splicing allow physicians now to treat genetic diseases. Tiny snippets of genetic material currently can be easily formed and can be inserted into the DNA code. Genetic cloning since Dolly has advanced with now over twenty animals cloned. Proteins produced by a disease state can be determined in the blood as markers of such diseases, and this information can lead to new therapies.

The life of a single cell organism is composed of a series of complex physical and biochemical processes with replication capabilities and associated
defense mechanisms to protect against environmental dangers. We know that
complex life evolved from simpler organisms; however, to answer the question of the origins of life, we are faced with a daunting task, so now we will
assess some of the possibilities.

1. *A single cell came together with the passage of time from DNA, RNA,*
   proteins, and enzymes, which were created in a chemical soup within a
   watery environment, somewhere by chance, after a long period of time.

The Earth dates back about 4.5 billion years and the earliest evidence of
life is somewhere between 3.5 and 4 billion years. The argument that time
will allow unusual events to occur is questionable when the amount of time
needed is many times greater than the life of the universe. The infinite monkey
theorem states that a monkey typing keys randomly would *eventually* write
Shakespeare's *Hamlet*. The chance of it occurring during a period of time,
even for thousands of orders of magnitude longer than the age of the universe,
is nearly zero. By the time one paragraph of text was formed, it would probably be more than the life of the universe. If the notion of predicting infre-
quent events seems unlikely, it is commonplace to then appeal to long periods
of time as a solution. However, models for the self-organization of life yield
probabilities far less than even every published probability statistical upper
bound and well beyond thousands of lifetimes of the universe. To form the
cell, one needs the rightly coded DNA for instructions, coordination of RNA,
proteins, enzymes, cell wall, and an energy unit even for the simplest cell;
however, some special physical environment, a combination of temperature,
pressure, and fluid, could significantly improve the improbable odds.

2. *Life was seeded from outer space. This is known as the Panspermia*
   Hypothesis.

The universe existed for about 10 billion years before the Earth, so it could
be possible that life took hold elsewhere in the universe, and then a meteorite
with life on board seeded our planet. The oldest known planet according to
NASA evidence in 2017 is 13 billion years old and is present in our Milky
Way. In 1998, two meteorites, Monahans and Zag, crashed into Earth, one
in Texas and the other near Morocco. They contained traces of organic matter including amino acids, hydrocarbons, and in addition, salt crystals with
water in them. The meteorites had been in our asteroid belt for billions of
years. Recently, Japan's spacecraft, Hayabusa2, along with a NASA craft,
OSIRIS-REx, have landed on the asteroids, Ryugu and Bennu respectively,

where the asteroids' rocks are undergoing sensor surveys. The hope is that the crafts will return collected samples, which will contain organic compounds and water. Hayabusa2 actually returned to Earth in December 2020 and OSIRIS-REx is scheduled to leave for home in April 2021. To date, there is only minimal evidence of an extraterrestrial life source, but it is possible these new probes or future probes will help us to understand the question about the origins of life on our planet.[2]

3. *Viruses Came First*

Most scientists believe that viruses came after cellular organisms because viruses generally need a cell to feed on. However, classes of giant MegaDNA viruses have been characterized recently and properties have been revealed that other viruses don't have. They do not need to capture just the host's replicating machine, but rather they have some replicating machinery of their own. For example, the Pithovirus discovered in the Siberian Permafrost around 2013 has been dormant for 30,000 years and has around 500 genes that can repair and replicate DNA structures. In comparison, the Influenza virus has about eight genes. Because of this discovery, some scientists say that the concept of the virus coming after the cell may not be correct. Only time will tell whether further evidence leads us in this direction, but the complexity of these viruses is quite extraordinary.[3]

4. *Hydrothermal Vents in the Sea Floor and Subterranean Life*

Hydrothermal vents in the sea floor have ideal conditions for chemical reactions to form because of warm temperatures and an aqueous environment. Some believe that the odds of life-sustaining molecules forming and conjoining are greatly improved in this environment.

Recent ongoing investigations of subterranean life about 5,000 meters or more below the ground may give new clues into the origin of life on Earth. Even in these most inhospitable regions below the Earth, life is present, but its sustaining energy is not oxygen.

Scientists estimate this subterranean biosphere is teeming with about twenty tons of microorganisms. Some of the organisms exist at the very edges of hospitable environmental conditions with little or no water and extreme heat. There is a current temperature maximum of 122 °C for life to exist, but researchers believe this record will be broken. Many species spend their lives bound to minerals, where they live, and the further study of their DNA, etc. should yield clues about why life wants to find a way to live despite enormous challenges. Will we find such life forms in other planets? Did life forms start in this subterranean environment, and then move upward and change markedly as they did? Most of the ideas here are highly speculative and science, as facts emerge, may narrow down the possibilities of the origin of life but ultimately the explanation of this origin if achieved may lead to a philosophical or logical quandary.[4]

NOTES

1. Schrodinger, Edwin, *What is Life?*, 1944.
2. Chang, Kenneth, *Asteroid*, 2020.
3. Legendre, Mathieu et al., *DNA*, 2014.
4. Mastin, L., *Hydrothermal Vents*, 2009.

Chapter 5

Riddle 4

Teleology and a Preordained Purpose in Our Lives

Teleology is an explanation of something based on its final form, goal, or purpose rather than previous causes. For example, Aristotle said that to understand an acorn it was best to look at its end purpose, which would be a fully-grown tree. To look at it scientifically, one would take a cause and effect approach. Where did it come from? What are its chemical and biologic constituents? Aristotle knew that powerful, transactional information resided at the end of this process. Modern science has discovered an intelligent set of instructions in the genetic materials, including DNA, that when present in the soil with the right environment, the little acorn eventually becomes a tree. Science makes its strides with logical causality, but teleology can sometimes point to information or intelligence built into the object of concern and leads the scientist in the correct direction.

Plato pointed out that the results of human activities could be based on purpose and not causality alone. He explained that Socrates was sitting in his prison cell not only because his tendons and ligaments held him but rather that his purpose or desire was to relax and sit. With human intelligence and emotion, choices can be made and purposes and goals can guide action. The social sciences attempt to make a causal connection with human activity, but the analysis improves when teleology is incorporated because purposes guide us. When it comes to studying groups of people or events, extra care needs to be made regarding teleological assessment since the purpose of groups and their ideas can be used to disenfranchise subgroups or other groups.

Teleology or preordained purpose in our lives questions the extent to which intelligence guides our material universe, our living spiritual universe, and our physical and mental evolution. We know that our world is in constant flux from the moment we are conceived. We know the universe is vast and our planet in comparison is just a speck. We understand, however, that our

genetic code contains a purpose; namely, our mental and physical development in a multitude of stages. Like the acorn, our genetic codes conjoined
from our parents to create an individual with the potential to think, love,
and work in society with purpose, a purpose that has developed over many
generations. Such an evolution could not occur if it were not for the chemical
basis of life that follows well-defined chemical and physical laws.

Thus, evolution does have a teleology, although not fully known, but while
the scientific causality picture of evolution is correct, it does not in principle
concern itself with this issue since it considers the physical laws to be a given.
Our world has an orderly process associated with it. If everything was completely random, life could never exist. In fact, nothing meaningful could exist.
The fundamental structure of our physical laws have a teleology of evolution
written in them and when one considers the moral and aesthetic order that
exits, the case for purpose is even stronger. Survival of the fittest could have
stopped with vegetation, but it did not because intrinsic to the physical laws
was the possibility of increased mobility and of increased information for the
organism. With the eventual evolution of rationality and morality, human life,
just as the acorn, intrinsically contained these possibilities.

The philosopher, Thomas Nagel, recently proposed a non-Darwinian
account of evolution similar to Bergson's and Whitehead's that incorporates
teleological laws to explain the existence of life, consciousness, rationality,
and objective value. He is in disagreement with those who see scientific
evolution as capable of a logical and consistent explanation without teleology while at the same time, he agrees with the scientific part of evolution.
However, Nagel viewed teleology as natural, not supernatural.[1]

Our human purpose in life depends on social order. Without the ordering
of moral, spiritual, and aesthetic values of individuals with respect to fellow
society members, our rational species would destroy itself. Even our history seems to have a purpose. Dramatic progress has occurred in education,
science, health, and longevity. While our political structures and societal
freedoms ebb and flow, we still can envision progress. Our world order and
knowledge have set the framework for growth. As mentioned in a previous
chapter, our advanced developmental knowledge may be detrimental because
of our scientific development of nuclear weapons or toxic biological agents.
A belief in an intelligent being as a source of the physical and aesthetic-moral
laws arises because we recognize that laws don't exist without a lawmaker,
and this, along with other factors, leads to a religious notion.

Religious beliefs, not necessarily institutionalized, in the history of mankind have existed and continue to exist in a majority of people because
as Alfred North Whitehead has said in his book *Religion In The Making*:
"The final principle of religion is that there is a wisdom in the nature of
things, from which flow our direction of practice, and our possibility of the

theoretical analysis of fact."[2] He then says that there are two main avenues for this belief, and one is in our reasoning abilities and our success in formulating fundamental theoretical scientific ideas. Secondly, our ability to discern aesthetic value and order in our relationships to others and to society goes well beyond anything that can be fully captured with words.

Purpose and meaning for each individual and all of mankind are fundamental to any truly religious experience. Of course, many religions throughout history have not successfully met this challenge, and some religious dogmas over the centuries have caused severe harm rather than good. While Du Bois-Reymond's riddle of purpose can in ultimate terms be approached and supported by the reasoning process and the moral order, its resolution fundamentally depends, at this time, on our faith based on our assessment and implementation of aesthetic value in our lives. We rely on experiencing love and justice.

Thornton Wilder's book *The Bridge of San Luis Rey* deals with a sudden tragedy where a bridge collapses and a number of people pass away. A friar, who investigates their lives and loves, questions this event. Why did this tragedy happen to these particular individuals and what did they have in common? In the end, no reason is found for their common fate, but the following quote, which is at the end of the book states: "There is a land of the living and a land of the dead and the bridge is love, the only survival, the only meaning."[3] Saint Thomas in his *Summa Theologica* addressed the nature of faith and the following condensed quote points to the primacy of love: "Faith must always remain a dark way, because the truth of faith cannot be grasped by the unaided workings of the human intellect for this requires the cooperation of the will. What sets the will in motion is love. While the intellect draws the soul to God it is the will (through love) that more perfectly attains to him."[4]

Neither philosophy nor science can fully solve the riddle of teleology or purpose, so faith is the guiding hand if one wants it. Will scientific progress or new facts or new events make our purpose clearer or more confusing in the future? Will a more advanced civilization contact us with more knowledge of our extraordinary existence? Will intelligent robots offer insight? Will men figure out how to backup their lives on computers, get new bodies and live for long periods, and cease to care about purpose? For now, this Du Bois-Reymond riddle is still not rationally fully answerable.

In the next section, we will look at Whitehead's philosophy in terms of purpose and teleology, which has been adapted by some Christian religions as process theology. The beauty of this construct by Whitehead is that it brings the advances in science in line with the philosophical quest for meaning in our lives. While not a proof, Whitehead's construct as a rational case for a caring, supernatural being, is strong and avoids the pitfalls of previous interesting "logical" proofs for God's existence. We will also look at the problem of evil in the world that tends to crush the religious experience and how that affects our faith.

NOTES

1. Nagel, Thomas, *Mind and Cosmos*, 2012.
2. Whitehead, Alfred North, *Religion*, 1926, 134.
3. Wilder, Thornton, *San Luis Rey*, 1983, 122.
4. Aquinas, Thomas, Summa, 2018.

Chapter 6

Process Philosophy and Theology

Prior to our discussion of the mysteries of consciousness and free will, we shall first discuss Process Philosophy and its impact on purpose and religion. Process Philosophy was created by Alfred North Whitehead at the beginning of the twentieth century during his tenure as a philosophy professor at Harvard University. Whitehead was born in England in the shore town of Ramsgate on the southeast coast, near where St. Augustine landed on a mission from the Pope in AD 597. Notably, the renowned artist, Vincent Van Gogh, also lived in Ramsgate around 1876. In Whitehead's youth, the aura of English history permeated the region and eventually led him in his early training to study history and the classics. When they were combined with his eventual math and science studies, he gained a unique philosophical breadth. He was a frail child but loved the outdoors especially by the seaside and he also spent considerable time outdoors with the family gardener with whom he kept in touch for many years.

Whitehead eventually became a professor of mathematics in England prior to going to Harvard. His work there included collaboration with Bertrand Russell, his student, on a now famous book entitled *Principia Mathematica* that dealt with the very foundation of mathematical theory. He also was interested in the physics of relativity, which had recently been developed by Einstein, and he proceeded to formulate it in a unique way, different but consistent with Einstein's. Whitehead brought the rigor of mathematics and science to the philosophical realm. He set out to include all elements of human life and physical reality into a scheme consistent with the current knowledge of science, the physical world, and the spiritual world, including man's consciousness and religious quests. I will attempt here to relate in a simple manner the important features. Two of his major books include

Process and Reality and *Religion in the Making* to which you can refer for further details.[1, 2]

Whitehead felt that in order to construct a theory of everything one needed to look at units of change or process as fundamental rather than just static concepts of being. Since we are in a constant state of flux, some essential elements are necessary for the effective transition from one unit to another. Somehow, the new "actual entity" evolves from the old one and becomes the precursor for the next. According to Whitehead, three underlying factors are needed in order to explain this process. These three elements are the eternal forms, creativity, and God. The eternal forms are all possible abstract objects or essences that can be conceived, similar to Plato's forms. A man, a boat, dark matter, and black holes are all conceptual forms. Even objects nonexistent at the time such as the concept of an internet existed as a potential form prior to its actual existence.

The second element is creativity. The world is constantly changing but in order to understand change, we need to invoke unchanging concepts. Some consistency even in change is necessary or else the world would be in a state of total disorder. Creativity is the act of connection between past actual entities, eternal forms, and our third element, God, to produce a new actual entity.[3]

The transformation from one actual entity to a new one means the integration of the past event with all possible forms under certain constraints imposed by God to form the new actual entity. Such integration is the role of creativity. For example, if we want to understand the transformation of a billiard ball from one moment to the next after being hit by the cue stick, the new actual entity depends on the initial position of the ball, the strength of the force exerted, the nature of the surface resistance, and the constraint that is Newton's laws of mechanics. For physical transformation, the laws are constrictive and/or probabilistic whereas in the conscious mind there is much more novelty and the introduction of values in reasoning choices. The constraining force here is the lure of God—the possibility of purposeful and harmonious moral change.

God allows free will within the constraints of physical laws; therefore, intentional evil exists, but God's lure aims to overcome such evil with good. Whitehead states of God: "He does not create the world, he saves it: or, more accurately, he is the poet of the world, with tender patience leading it by his vision of truth, beauty, and goodness."[4] God also is aware of time and his vision is one outside of time, of a final harmony, yet he suffers with each of us, or shares in our peace and harmony as time evolves:

"The depths of his existence lie beyond the vulgarities of praise or of power.
He gives to suffering its swift insight into values which can issue from it. He

is the ideal companion who transmutes what has been lost into a living fact within his own nature. He is the mirror which discloses to every creature its own greatness."[5]

A number of questions arise from this philosophy. Some people might ask—why do we have to invoke God and teleology in this process and isn't evolution a full explanation? Since there is a reality where all the actual entities will perish, Whitehead believed it is essential to have a nontemporal being who can oversee the process and the possibilities. This is analogous to the frames in a movie where each frame perishes, but the whole film needs to have someone in charge of all of the frames. Evolution is in reality constrained by physical laws and the necessity of survival; however, Whitehead points out that each actual occasion has both a physical and a mental pole. As consciousness arose in different species and with it emotions and eventually rationality, survival depended on these mental aspects. Animals needed to care for their young and often utilized the talents of each member, and fostered loyalty to the pack.

With human reasoning, concepts of law and order and justice become essential for survival. Evolution moved in this direction because of an inherent tendency present at the beginning of the universe. The leaps from the physical world to the world of consciousness, emotion, and rationality were huge and could not have occurred without appropriate physical laws and intelligence that a priori enabled such changes. Whitehead's theory is not modern day creationism but rather recognition that an intelligent force underlies all those beautiful physical theories and underlies gradations of values that emerge in communities. Our basic moral laws are real and consistent and comprised of an underlying intelligence, which gives them a physical order and the potential for moral and aesthetic order.

Another question that arises is the question of evil. Whitehead said that philosophies in general were shipwrecked on the problem of evil. If one has an omnipotent God, then how can he allow such evil in the world to exist? Whitehead's philosophy tries to get around this problem by making God immanent and dependent on the world and by keeping him as the ideal lure for harmony and morality in the world. He guides the world towards his vision of moral and aesthetic beauty. Whitehead's philosophy attempted to incorporate knowledge of science as well as aspects of other human endeavor such as history, morality, and religion. Materialists who just look at physical science as the only reality miss the true nature and complexity of human existence.

Our current scientific knowledge confronts the fact that at the beginning of the Big Bang, all physical laws end, and we have no idea what comes before that point or even if that is a valid question. Process theology would argue that God without the physical universe would be meaningless. If God as a creator is outside the universe and set it all in motion, then God would allow evil to exist. Therefore, Whitehead is right that all philosophies are shipwrecked on the problem of evil. Traditionally, God allows evil as a necessity for our free will to exist, but Whitehead shifts the burden of evil onto creativity, which allows all possibilities and forms (free will), and God's lure helps to constrain them.

The physical world is inherently a potential source of evil for individual entities. Our physical frailty is impacted by all sorts of evils from tornadoes, earthquakes, and all kinds of trauma to pathogens, poisons, and psychic trauma. The temporal process itself, however, has inherent evil as seen by Whitehead in the following quote: "The ultimate evil in the temporal world is deeper than any specific evil, it lies in the fact that the past fades, that time is a 'perpetual perishing.'"[6] Process, with our finite existence, inherently involves some loss since with each step our past becomes an abstraction never fully regained. Our lives are continuously fractured.

On a moral level, mankind's misuse of freedom, selfishness, and lack of knowledge has caused the world tremendous atrocities sometimes even in the name of religion. Many people have been subjected to severe violence, or have witnessed such an event and have often observed a member of their family give up on God or even blame him. If God is by nature unceasingly good as Whitehead said and he suffers with us, then man can worship him as holy and sacred in both good and horrible times. God does not change the physical laws to create goodness but through rationality and wisdom, we can use other laws to block existing evils. For example, when a medical drug is developed with the ability to kill an organism that causes pneumonia, this utilizes the physical properties of matter and the laws of chemistry to combat a potentially deadly bacterium.

It is important to remember that the actual entities are in an interactive process with a sea of external actual entities, and each actual entity is interconnected. We rely on and depend on each other in the process. The concept of minds as independent substances leads to a private world of morals.

When people begin to think solely in terms of "I made myself a success," they forget all those events and people that helped them along the way. That interdependence and cooperation is an innate consequence of process metaphysics and theology. God is the "soul of the universe," and we influence him, and he affects us. Whitehead says of God: "He is that element in virtue of which our purposes extend beyond values for ourselves to values for others."[7]

Process involves time, but God is always with us. Whitehead's following statement poetically captures the complex reality of our world: "The world is at once a passing shadow and a final fact. The shadow is passing into the fact, so as to be constitutive of it; and yet the fact is prior to the shadow. There is a kingdom of heaven prior to the actual passage of actual things, and there is the same kingdom finding its completion through the accomplishment of this passage."[8]

We live unlike other animals in a spiritual as well as a physical world. We have language to deal with abstract forms and reasoning powers to uncover the reality of our relationships to each other and our physical world. Our stories and music are rich in emotions. We worry about past decisions and fear our future ones. Each of us ultimately stands alone with wonderment at our finite changing existence. The order and nature of our spiritual world implies the universe with its quite rigid physical laws and its moral and aesthetic possibilities was imbued with a spirit from the beginning, and will continue to be this way after our existence here. Our relationship to and union with this nontemporal aesthetic spirituality helps us to live our lives here for the just benefit of others and ourselves. The mechanism of such union is the utilization of our spiritual energy in prayer to aid us in our decisions and actions. The flow of this spiritual energy must be based on a genuine open mind and open heart while not constrained solely by external dogma.

The above paragraph describes a general notion of religion. In practice, many religions have helped human progress while others have distorted religion into an evil end. As Whitehead has said, "Religion is by no means necessarily good . . . The God with whom you have made terms may be the God of destruction, the God who leaves in his wake the loss of the greater reality."[9]

Whitehead speaks of objective immortality for actual occasions in that they live on in other actual occasions and in a special way in God's nature. Whitehead's God is a personal one because his lure is aesthetic and moral. This personal nature is consistent with Whitehead's metaphysical construct and with our finer religious notions and intuitions. God needs us and we need him as he transforms and weaves our actions into permanent significance. He is the judge but more importantly the friend and redeemer who guides us in the notions of right and wrong, justice and peace, love, and eternity. The importance of our lives and actions within him are, as Whitehead said, "beyond our imagination to conceive." Some attempts at describing them are "shocking and profane," and yet without his union with us our activities are "a passing whiff of insignificance."[10]

NOTES

1. Whitehead, A. N., *Process*, 1929.
2. Whitehead, A.N., *Religion*, 1926.
3. McPherson, Jeffrey A., *Creativity*, 1998.

4. Whitehead, A.N., 1929, 348.
5. Whitehead, A.N., 1926, 135.
6. Whitehead, A.N., 1929, 340.
7. Whitehead, A.N., 1926, 8.
8. Whitehead, A.N., 1926, 72.
9. Whitehead, A.N., 1926, 9.
10. Hosinski, Thomas, *Stubborn Fact*, 1993, 203.

Chapter 7

Riddles 5 and 6

Origin of Sensation, Consciousness, Reasoning, and Language

As we continue on our quest to understand the seven riddles, we now look at the origin of sensation, consciousness, reasoning, and language. The physical laws of the world allow for individuality by granting spatial separation, chemical structures, and forces suitable for genetic and epigenetic evolution. Evolution of various organisms from single cells and viruses to plants and trees that take nutrients from the soil along with sunlight and water eventually led to mammals with complex sensory organs, increased mobility, and consciousness. Consciousness can be defined as concerned awareness and characterized by sensation, emotion, and volition. Consciousness allowed for awareness of other individuals and their emotional states and this increased protection from danger. With the evolutionary development of human beings, language and reasoning suddenly flourished.

SENSATION AND CONSCIOUSNESS

Du Bois-Reymond believed the origin of sensation was just as complicated as the origin of emotion and volition. Not only were the sense organs involved, but also the mind had an active process in interpretation. Henri Bergson observed that it is a false notion that matter has the hidden power to produce representations in us. In actuality, the mind is actively involved in the sensations because our knowledge of the external world is relative knowledge based on previous information and interpretation. It is not disinterested knowledge. The mind analyzes and uses intuition instead of basing its understandings on just an external perspective. Our constructed image is a virtual reality.[1]

Sensation, emotion, and volition as components in the development of consciousness were a giant, complex leap, which clearly took many generations. From a mechanistic perspective, they are not technically comprehensible at this time; however, various theories exist including the necessity of invoking quantum theory in order to understand them. As we have alluded to in previous chapters, there is, from the beginning, a modeling, intelligent force in the universe that shares awareness, knowledge, and emotion, and inherently guides our spiritual evolution. The possibility that our conscious self-awareness is just understood based on a random survival model, which happens to create an intelligent, spiritual being is not coherent with the fundamental notion of process as described by Whitehead. For Whitehead, God exists as a nontemporal being that aesthetically and morally helps to constrain the evolutionary process.

LANGUAGE AND RATIONALITY

The development of language and rationality was a momentous leap in evolution. Did a rational world exist prior to this evolutionary step? We can answer this question in the affirmative because humans would eventually understand the rational physical laws that existed long before mankind's presence. Logic, as per Whitehead's philosophy from the last chapter, implies some nontemporal entity must constrain the physical force possibilities; otherwise, there would be chaos and we could not exist.

Is there an evolutionary advantage to language and rationality? Yes, potentially because it provides for problem solving and for knowledge being transferred easily from generation to generation. However, with rationality comes choices and with that comes some form of free will (which will be discussed in the next chapter in more detail). With our choices and free will, our evolution can get unpredictable. Man now has the ability with one wrong decision to annihilate the entire planet.

THE MORAL CONSTRAINTS AND LURE

The ability for social and moral development is reinforced by its potential survival benefit, but unlike the physical laws, they are not absolute. As with the physical laws, one can ask whether the moral aesthetic law existed prior to mankind's appearance? We know the physical science laws predated man's existence. In the case of aesthetic, moral laws, we can tell from the time before man that nonhuman primates cared for and protected their children and their group members. Based on a statistical analysis of the tenth to the twenty-fourth power number of planets, we know there is a significant likelihood that many planets exist with intelligent life elsewhere in the universe, and probably predate us, and some may have grown with greater success toward a goal of aesthetic and moral order. Therefore, the notion of Whitehead's moral constraints or lure probably predates our temporal human existence.

Once the physical laws and constraints allowed for living beings to immerse in a spiritual plane, evolution was further constrained by a vision of a universal harmony and beauty despite the enormous challenges each person and generation could face. We know the constraints are constantly being tested, for mankind's decisions are often irrationally based and as mentioned above, one person's irrational or immoral behavior could result in the extinction of our world. Is the aesthetic lure sufficiently strong for mankind and is man capable of successfully exercising free will in a period where our technology is advanced beyond our morality?

God is the fulfillment of being; therefore, evolution is constrained by physical and spiritual laws. Could one invoke only physical constraints? No, because once we have beings with some choices, their decisions are complex and further evolution cannot be predictable without considering the spiritual reality. The spiritual reality also can cause epigenetic physical changes.

Contrasting spiritual lure towards greater aesthetic harmony is the concept of original sin, which reflects our individual selfishness. Human consciousness promotes individual self-preservation, and a cross is formed between the self and others. Unlike the heart, the kidneys, and the intestines, the brain has a non-mechanical function; namely, the abstraction and manipulation of the external forms and then the assimilation of them into a coherent evolving concept of self in a changing environment, taking actions that are hopefully just. The lure towards aesthetic beauty can easily crumble under the weight of human desire, and this fact has always been humbling for all of us.

ROBOTIC MAN

We are a lot closer to understanding human consciousness now than in the 19th century. To give a robotic system even a simple level of consciousness without animal brain tissue would probably mean employing futuristic sophisticated computers, possibly quantum computers, using machine self-learning algorithms. These calculations might then integrate with synthetic neural units made of biologic type materials. It could be a long time until this happens but if it does happen, it will not necessarily diminish mankind. However, if we could somehow recreate human consciousness and reasoning, we would face a truly new dangerous frontier where human survival would depend upon an improvement in the moral integrity of men and women.

LANGUAGE'S ORIGIN

Animals communicate with one another often with simple visual signals or grunts but with insects, communal activities are already genetically programmed as in the case of bees. Humans learn to speak by exposure to the speech of others. How did the first human language come into being?

One hypothesis is that natural evolution at some point led to the acquisition of language. Brain size increased significantly when evolving from Homo erectus to Homo sapiens and this change could explain the development of language. Memory storage is necessary for thought and language, and it is probable that this increased as brain size grew along with brain redistribution to language areas. Homo sapiens began evolving about 150,000 years ago and eventually supplanted other species.

A religious hypothesis of divine creation has portrayed humans from the start with an innate capacity to speak. This hypothesis cannot be proven or disproven; however, it is not consistent with gradual but major changes in brain development over long periods as mentioned above.

THE FIRST LANGUAGES

How did the first language evolve from forms that were more primitive?[2] Numerous hypotheses exist that are based on natural sounds. For example, the "ding-dong" hypothesis describes how boom might mean an explosion, crash may mean thunder, and tun-tun might mean a beating heart. This would be a limited vocabulary but it could have been a start. The "pooh-pooh" hypothesis is based on automatic vocal responses to emotional reactions such as wow, ha-ha, or ouch. The "bow wow" hypothesis originated from imitation—barking sound for a dog, a meow for a cat, and an oink for a pig, etc. The "ta-ta" hypothesis explains how lip movements imitate hand gestures. Ta-ta happens when you wave your hand when you say goodbye.

Others see language arising because of a community's needs. The warning hypothesis is based on help or run in response to an attack by an animal. Other words may have originated for different, common situations such as dig or clean, etc. The "yo-he-ho" hypothesis considers language evolving from cooperative effort, such as moving a great stone, military marching chants, or rowing chants. The lying hypothesis says that language developed as a means to deceive by contrasting reality with selfish interests.

Each of these hypotheses falls short in terms of their limited scope, but all of them rest upon the fact that man had the ability to think about concepts abstractly, store them in memory to retrieve them later, and had the vocal apparatus to pronounce many different ideas. Interposed with this is the logic of thought that is necessary to develop rational conclusions and have appropriate grammatical constructs. Man had surpassed the primates mysteriously with language and logic.

Was there a single, original language? This probably was not the case since local customs and values would have predominated. Languages that are older and known are just as complex, if not more complex, than current languages.

LANGUAGE AND PROGRESS

Language is a way to communicate abstract ideas and gives rise to social abstract notions, which includes evil, justice, kindness, cruelty, love, hate, mortality and immortality, and also deity and the devil. With this language, politics and governments were created to write laws. Within the constraints of laws, individual freedoms are tested. Morality and faith brought forth the Golden Rule, and poverty was confronted. Fear of other societies led to wars, and these wars led to anti-war groups. Technology grows as man's successful reasoning becomes codified. Language is becoming more and more abstract and removed from facts.

THE FUTURE OF LANGUAGE AND REASON

So what is the future of language and reasoning? Just as we only have a rough guess of the origins of language and reason, we can only guess about the future. Language is structured to convey reality by being constrained from Aristotelian logic; however, emotions can easily overtake logic. With mass media organizations and unscrupulous politicians twisting language in favor of one group over another, language can fail the truth. The media in our complicated modern life also tends to minimize innovative ideas and important contributions of ordinary people in the society in favor of media stars and politicians. When this is combined with the continued power of violence as the ultimate arbitrator, language becomes crippled. Mankind must teach their future generations about data and information overload, but they will also have to think globally and be able to ferret out the truth from constant attempts to distort language and reason.

The twentieth century saw the horrors of the Nazis propaganda machine and its terrible consequences. Will the twenty-first century with all the technology and instant communications of print, video, photo, and audio be able to prevent or enhance the distortion of language and reason? Will the horrors of the twenty-first century exceed the twentieth? Will the world resist the temptation to use their weapons of power and annihilation in this century and instead commit to logical arbitration of differences among groups? To what extent will science, as the ultimate arbiter of our physical realm, continue to be marginalized by distortions of language and logic in dealing with climate change and individual safety? Will individual worth expressed through the language of spiritual values, poetry, and the arts be sacrificed at the altar of financial or special interest gain?

NOTES

1. Bergson, Henri, *Matter and Memory*, 1910.
2. Harris, Roy Ed., *Origin of Language*, 1996.

Chapter 8

Riddle 7

Free Will

There is no doubt that mankind's choices in life are constrained in many ways. A person doesn't choose to exist; it just happens. One does not choose his parents, their degree of wisdom, or their possessions. At first, one usually does not have much influence regarding his initial education or his health care. All of us are constricted as well by the limitations of the material world, including the limitations of our physical bodies. We have no real control over our limited life expectancy or over what are "Acts of God" events in our lives. With our development, we begin to make choices and clearly have some freedom in relation to most of those choices. One might argue that one's choices are influenced by all the factors mentioned earlier, which would be true, but one can still choose.

Much has been written and argued about free will for centuries.[1] Aristotle believed that mature individuals usually make choices after deliberating about different available means to their ends, drawing on a somewhat rational approach. He believed if one consistently chose well, a virtuous character could develop in time. He understood that choices were dependent on previous choices and outside influences affected these choices, but he saw moral responsibility as inseparable from making choices.

Saint Augustine believed that man's misuse of freedom, not God, is the reason for men's evil acts in the world. He believed that the human will has been corrupted through original sin and salvation or success usually only occurs through hard work and the grace of God. St. Augustine is attributed with saying, *"Pray as though everything depended on God. Work as though everything depended on you."* This prayer recognizes that the moral spiritual order comes to us from God but that the hard work of implementing it depends on us. Morality is a key point in free will. Truths do not need to be told but without objectivity, a society of free wills built on lies will collapse. Free will can be thought of having the following requirements:

1. To have free will, one has the power of self-determination, thus the freedom to make another choice. If one has a mental illness, one may not have that ability. If a gun is pointed at one's head, a real choice may not be possible.
2. A free individual is morally responsible and can be subject to punishment.
3. The final requirement is compatibilism, the thesis that free will is compatible with some element of determinism.

However, the belief by some of a pure physical determinism is not a good argument because modern physics is incompatible with pure determinism. This was a common notion in the 19th century when Newton's laws held sway, but the advent of quantum theory has evaporated those arguments of a pure physical determinism. I think we can safely say that from the perspective of a given individual free of illness or coercion and with all the limitations of his personal experiences, he is still capable of making a choice. This is all that is meant and should be meant by the term, free will. Philosophers will continue to argue about how much free will we have. Based on one's background one might have a reasonable guess of what choice a person might make but that person is still free to make a choice.

The background we inherit is like quasi-predestination that we have to contemplate as we move forward. When viewing others we need to see that their view of the world is based on their quasi-predestination and both of us have to reckon with this idea. Religious predestination came from similar notions combined with the belief that God was omniscient and knew a priori who would and would not be saved. Process theory attempted to avoid that conundrum because God is a fundamental support in our temporal world and is affected by our free will choices. While he is non-temporal, he intimately lives with our choices.

Process theory in some ways shows what free will really means. It is the transition between the changes of actual occasions involved in decision-making; the previous occasion is melded with all associated occasions, creativity, and God's lure, in order to come to a decision. The important point is that each decision is affected by the total environment and the next choice is dependent on the previous one and the new environment, etc. Interdependence in a given choice is complex. A person initially makes complicated decisions based on those who raised him, those who love him, his innate genetics, his learning, and his health and on and on, yet he still is the one who is free to decide and is responsible. In decision-making, one needs to realize all the factors that influence us and realize our narrow view.

I believe that free will is a riddle that is and always will be hard to fully unravel; however, it is not in the same category as the other riddles because it is logical and complex and is ultimately dependent on the definition of what we mean by free will. Since we can and do make choices that affect our lives, let us now move on to what have been called the "Second Tier Riddles." These are the practical applications of our interpretation of the Du Bois-Reymond riddles.

NOTE

1. Pink, Thomas, *Free Will*, 2004.

Chapter 9

The Second Tier Riddles

The second tier, the how to riddles, that mankind faces are the potential practical applications of the beliefs one develops about the previous seven philosophical riddles. We list and discuss them here usually with a brief comment alluding to their potential future solvability. A lot has been written on each of these ideals, and they involve enormous complexity as reflected in the literature. Following this analysis will be a discussion of the connection between the two sets of riddles.[1]

1. Elimination of violence and war in society.
2. Elimination of illness, accidents, addictions, and an increase in a healthy longevity.
3. Elimination of racial, religious, economic, sexual and class prejudice.
4. Elimination of illiteracy and allow a fundamental critical thinking and basic moral (not religious) educational curriculum for all.
5. Universal social service networks for those in dire need of help.
6. The development of truly democratic and just republics that encourage freedom, compassion, justice, and responsibility.
7. Create socially responsive and international free enterprise business, educational, and research institutions.

1. ELIMINATION OF VIOLENCE AND WAR IN SOCIETY

War and violence has been a steady reality throughout history, and the riddle of how to end these problems has not been solved. Violence within a given society in modern times is somewhat constrained if one has a morally educated populace and if just laws exist and are enforced, but unfortunately human emotion can trigger rage and overcome rationality. Moral values can be absent or rationalized away. As G.K. Chesterton had pointed out, the self and its selfishness can represent mankind's original sin, and consequently utopian hopes are usually dashed.[2]

What can give us hope that violence can be eliminated in the future? New technologies open up potential support for aiding society with identifying those in need of social services. Facebook and other social networks have records of each user's political inclination, and this information has been made available and inappropriately exploited by political groups, some of whom are foreign powers. However, these types of services with large amounts of data can also help those in need of social services. School administrators and counselors could collect and use their own data from a school social site to monitor how the students feel about school and pinpoint concerns such as bullying and despair and respond appropriately. Video conferencing programs can allow social services to monitor clients at a lower cost as well as bring medical expertise, telemedicine, to remote places.

Education, as in riddle four, has the potential and should teach students about human emotions and prepare young people for possibly turbulent times in relationships and in work environments. The "separation of church and state" should not preclude conversations about dealing with the stresses and the moral conundrums that arise with growing up. We need to do better in our K-12 classrooms. Along with teaching math and science, we need to teach critical thinking. Critical thinking can make an enormous difference in regards to all aspects of our emotional, rational, and spiritual needs in life. Public school teachers need to be trained to carry out such a mission while at the same time respecting students' belief systems.

Improved education and social services (riddle five) will help eliminate violence and war, but weapons of war should not be allowed in the hands of mentally unstable individuals or those individuals with a record of threats or violence and if these sales are not totally banned, they should at least be heavily regulated. The entire criminal justice system should be modernized with appropriate enforcement and incarceration policies that focus on all forms of violence and focus less on individual drug-related sentencing. White collar and corporate crimes need to be addressed with more substantive appropriate penalties.

War depends on two or more societies with different values and viewpoints where one or more sees the need to use power and violence to control the actions of another. Reasons for justifying war vary, and they can often be easily rationalized. Even when we are attacked, we need to think of long-term solutions, not just an immediate military response.

We live in an age of instant communication, which is potentially good and bad. Sudden notions of an imminent nuclear attack as occurred in Hawaii in 2017 could be disastrous; however, increasingly complex communications and travel between the peoples of different countries may be one key for keeping peace in the future. Continued economic integrations with other governments and united efforts in the face of tragedies, such as hurricanes and infectious diseases, should also be helpful. Nuclear control and disarmament of the superpowers and smaller countries is possible only if a rational formulation can be forged. The consequences of not doing so could be horrendous. A rogue group with access to nuclear weapons has become a real possibility and constant monitoring will be needed to prevent this scenario from becoming a reality. Global economic coordination and assistance of smaller, poorer nations should also help. With the superhuman power of weapons, nuclear and biologic, we need to solve the problem of war before we are annihilated.

2. ELIMINATION OF ILLNESS, ACCIDENTS, ADDICTIONS, AND AN INCREASE IN A HEALTHY LONGEVITY

Illness is one area where we have made significant strides. We have improved people's quality of life, and we have helped them to live longer. Progress in cardiology in the past forty years has been amazing because of prevention and intervention for coronary artery disease and for valvular heart conditions. Surgery has become safer and less of a stress on the patient, such as in laparoscopic procedures. Cancer therapies have improved because of biotechnological advances. Strokes can sometimes be stopped if they are detected early enough. However, a lot of progress still has to be made on numerous illnesses that are resistant to treatment, which includes many cancers and neurological conditions. With time, it is conceivable that most problems will be classified as preventable or chronic conditions; however, new illnesses will arise. Our genetic makeup is an important factor in our susceptibility to diseases and will eventually be routinely modifiable.

Accidents are tragic and safer cars have helped to decrease the number of car accidents significantly over the past forty years, and current technology should continue to progress to the point where the risk becomes less than five percent of what it is now. Meanwhile, trauma teams have progressed from the time of the television show M*A*S*H, and many people are alive today who would have died from similar traumas seventy years ago. Inspections and enforcement of water, food, drugs, and airlines for safety by the appropriate agencies seems to be getting worse, and needs to get back into compliance with the high standards of the recent past. Much hope for future progress and success in these areas still exists in both the short and long term.

Addiction to drugs and alcohol has increased substantially in the past few years, especially in our young adults. The reason for this is multifactorial. The economy is one reason because younger people have not had the opportunities that previous generations have enjoyed in terms of finding meaningful employment. In addition, the moral constraints of our communities have diminished overall. Other addictions such as gambling can also be a strain on the young and their families. Progress means better education and better societal help in terms of employment and social avenues for the young. What is needed is that the will of the people must be exerted to encourage government and businesses to invest in elements of society that are unable to adapt to a rapidly changing world. Chances of success in the short term are probably poor since the society and the media tends to be uninterested in those who are marginalized. The long-term outlook is fair.

Aligned with longevity is the question of immortality. The natural life span is limited by genetics, and it would be an incredible task to work a way around the problem. One problem that also arises is that living a long time coupled with the limitations of old age would not necessarily result in a happy elderly existence. Another issue is the potentially severe adverse effects of the ensuing population explosion, making the support of the elderly a decreased priority as resources become limited. Climate change could curtail life expectancy as natural disasters proliferate and new bacterial and viral infections can more easily arise in society as the global mean temperature rises. The recent wildfires in Australia and California along with increasingly potent tropical storms plus rising ocean levels and melting ice caps all point to a transformation of the natural order by man-made emissions, which work against longevity and the quality of life. Similarly, the recent severe outbreak of Covid-19 portends of major peril for future pandemics related to climate or population issues.

The deleterious effects of the drug problem, among young adults in the USA, caused a drop in life expectancy for this group. Riddle four below, universal critical moral education, also needs a solution in order to help promote longevity. However, scientific progress regarding longevity should continue slowly to progress as our understanding of the relationship between genetic and epigenetic factors improves. Despite these problems, the chances for slow but continual improvement is fair to good if societies are willing to pay for new research and provide medical care and social services for their people.

3. ELIMINATION OF RACIAL, RELIGIOUS, ECONOMIC, SEXUAL AND CLASS PREJUDICE

The nature of prejudice finds its basis in fear and irrationality. We have made great strides in a positive direction with each new generation. We have to learn to live with people who look or think differently from ourselves. Generally, entire groups are difficult to characterize and have large differences within their populations. Each individual should be judged in terms of integrity, honesty, and capacity for caring.

For progress to continue a cooperation of educational, religious institutions, and media outlets constantly need to guard their discussions so that entire groups are treated fairly and not disparaged. A chance of some success exists in this area, but it depends on our ability to differentiate the abstract from the specific. Demonization of one group as completely bad is much too general, and it attributes nonhuman qualities to that group. This kind of abstraction misses the struggles that each individual endures.

Most of the people in every nation, despite some of their leaders, want to be safe and have health, freedom, and safety for their children and grandchildren. Politics and personal gain often pollutes our conversation, and they must be called out by the media, educational, religious and business institutions. Tolerance is another aspect that is necessary in societal discourse. A group may believe that gay marriage is wrong, but they should not dehumanize or injure gay or transgender individuals. Similarly, on difficult and complex issues such as gun control and abortion, strong beliefs are held by both sides, but one needs to put aside his or her prejudices and reexamine these issues in a critical and ethical way. A society incapable of reducing the roughly thirty-two thousand deaths per year by guns is not a healthy society. Existing creative ways of assisting young people can markedly reduce the approximately eight hundred thousand abortions performed yearly in the USA without the elimination of Roe v. Wade.

This practical riddle can be solved with education and critical thinking, and this method of resolution would go a long way toward solving all of the second tier riddles. This is because with knowledge and discourse combined with moral integrity, compromises can follow. The chances of this happening in the short term are poor but in the long term, it is possible.

4. ELIMINATION OF ILLITERACY AND ALLOW A FUNDAMENTAL CRITICAL THINKING AND BASIC MORAL (NOT RELIGIOUS) EDUCATIONAL CURRICULUM FOR ALL

We have already alluded to the importance of education, and it is essential for society, especially a democratic society, to have superior education in order to succeed. As of 2017, thirty-two million Americans can't read. Some African countries still have illiteracy rates of seventy-five percent. A lot of work needs to be done. Education is especially important today because of the fast pace of technology. Continuous learning about new job opportunities and how to fulfill them is required. Moral education is essential in order to keep the fabric of the society sustainable. Critical thinking is important to counteract the manipulations in social media and the ones that advertisers use to push their agendas. Critical thinking is also very important in the ever-increasing dependence of all aspects of society on complex technology and computer systems.

Morality is the backbone of any society. In general, just and fair laws existed in America in the 20th century that did not allow the rich to get a pass on the justice system. No payoffs were allowed for political favors or as a way of getting someone out of jail. We have been a beacon of hope for those in other countries, especially in the post-World War II era when we helped Europe with the Marshall plan. Overall, we kept our commitments, and the world looked to us as we led the way. Our leadership and word was trusted because our morality and credibility were paramount. We need continuing moral education in corporations, small businesses, and especially in government. We can and must make progress in this area but the short-term outlook looks uncertain.

5. UNIVERSAL SOCIAL SERVICE NETWORKS FOR THOSE IN DIRE NEED OF HELP

As societies increase in size, the number of people who fall through the cracks grows and a strong societal safety net is essential. Technologies as mentioned above allow instant communication and visualization throughout the world, and international groups should work together to help communities that need assistance. Some people frown on anyone who takes assistance from a charity or the government. In this country, some early Protestant sects believed that prosperity was a sign of spiritual success. Today some politicians rage about the need to cut back on food stamps and school meals. To take away a meal from a child who comes from a family currently unable to care adequately for him is cruel and "penny wise, pound foolish."

6. THE DEVELOPMENT OF TRULY DEMOCRATIC AND JUST REPUBLICS THAT ENCOURAGE FREEDOM, COMPASSION, JUSTICE, AND RESPONSIBILITY

The creation of just democratic republics worldwide seems to be diminishing. The internet and media networks are utilized more effectively by the rich and powerful despite the fact of worldwide usage. The American story of justice and freedom while not perfect has always been an inspiration for other countries to emulate and if America loses its moral leadership, the world will be set back.

We need to encourage freedom, compassion, justice, and responsibility— basic values enshrined in the hopes of our founding fathers. Thus, the chances of success in this case are currently poor but in the long term they are fair to good because mankind will presumably become more educated and value each soul as much as the collective group.

7. CREATE SOCIALLY RESPONSIVE AND INTERNATIONAL FREE ENTERPRISE BUSINESS, EDUCATIONAL, AND RESEARCH INSTITUTIONS

A free flow of ideas and activities in a society means businesses must be free to develop their products, but they also have a serious responsibility to society. Car and airline makers need to consider safety but so do most companies. Profit should not be their only goal; they need to look at the welfare of the society. Media companies and social media sites have not done a good job of policing their content. Companies need to be penalized when they fail and rewarded when they succeed, which also requires a functioning United States Congress. Educational institutions need to play a more active role in their graduates' future jobs by offering guidance for several years after graduation as part of their services. Research institutions need to ensure ethical standards of conduct in research and fair treatment of those in training or part-time roles. Research is the backbone of progress and economic leadership and must be supported by the government. This riddle has a poor chance of being solved successfully in the short term and a better chance in the long term.

How are these riddles connected to our previous fundamental riddles? They are intertwined with the fundamental philosophical riddles because of the interconnected way our world exists, our purpose and progress as global people, and the uniqueness of every family and every individual's soul. If this perspective is taken, then hope for progress in these practical riddles can happen. If one concludes that the answers to the philosophical riddles means that our lives lack freedom and a meaningful purpose, then how can we expect one to see a reason for contributing to one's community or envision a real future?

The hope is that one perceives in the fundamental riddles a spiritual world of value and purpose where love and caring exist. Such an answer could be thought of as your "religion." As Whitehead says in *Religion in the Making*, "Your character is developed according to your faith. . . . Religion is force of belief cleansing the inward parts."[3] With that fundamental definition, it doesn't demand a deity, a congregation, or an extended dogma. He then says, "In its solitariness the spirit asks, What, in the way of value, is the attainment of life? And it can find no such value till it has merged its individual claim with that of the objective universe. Religion is world-loyalty."[4]

Once your initial answer to the riddles of the universe includes value beyond the self, then an element of world loyalty is introduced. The ratio of the arms of the cross between the other and the self that one creates reflects your world loyalty. If someone believes only in the importance of his or herself, then there is no world loyalty and if only he or she and his or her family are all that matters, then one has a sadly limited type of world loyalty.

NOTES

1. Kaku, Michio, *The Future*, 2018.
2. Chesterton, Gilbert K., *Heritics*, 1909.
3. Whitehead, Alfred N., *Religion*, 1926, 7.
4. Whitehead, Alfred N., 1926, 8.

Chapter 10

Final Thoughts on the Riddles

A lot has happened in nearly a century and a half since Emil Du Bois-Reymond lectured on the seven riddles of the universe in 1872 and while major progress has been made on some of the riddles, they have not been solved. In regards to the origin of matter and motion, science has marched along with amazing strides; however, we are left with clear problems, some of which linger in the philosophical realm without any hope of a scientific solution. Why do matter and energy exist at all? Is string theory the ultimate basis of matter? What happened during the Big Bang's origin before the laws of physics existed? What does it mean to be outside of time? Why does matter follow laws? Most of these questions are not scientifically answerable because any logical precursor would need another reasonable precursor.

In the case of the origin of life, the complexity of going from inorganic matter to cellular organisms is improbable based on chance alone and is not provable until someone recreates it in a lab in a stepwise fashion or evidence emerges for life being seeded from elsewhere in the universe. While evolution is well grounded in comparative genetics, we have made the case that teleology needs to be considered rather than just random genetic mutations since the universe is imbued with intelligence, and this is a guide in the process. For example, in making early life certain key factors were necessary including energy sources: (sunlight), solvent (water), and basic carbon and inorganic chemicals; otherwise, all the chance encounters would be worthless. Evolution inherits a physical world capable of supporting life. Similarly, during the evolution of species, random genetic changes need to move towards gathering more knowledge or logic in order to protect species of increasing complexity.

As an example, let us look at an amoeba. It has no specialized sense receptors but if it moves into a very acidic region, it then reflexively moves back away. The development of this genetic set of changes has an evolutionary advantage of protecting the amoeba. It has a built in simple logic gate. Namely, if it senses an acidic environment, it moves away from it. Of course, the development of complex sensory receptors requires many genetic changes aimed at sharpening these receptors. For example, in mammals, the visual environment is perceived with amazing clarity. The species needs environmental knowledge to help them with protection. In addition, the complex sensory organs of mammals, unlike the simple reflex of the amoeba, need a brain to analyze and interpret the information. Much more logical programming is necessary.

The point is that the usually effective random mutations, which lead to acquiring logical knowledge, have to be in a small subset of all mutations. Thus, teleology, which guides this subset, is built into all of the intelligible physical laws that emerge from the Big Bang and allow for evolution through its software. This then allows for a lure towards more intelligent, rational, and potentially moral creatures. The survival of the fittest notion is also beyond the physical realm just as a software program has a fundamental non-physical information quality. Our physical world is an atomized type world where individual entities can exist within all of the connected entities in the universe. Evolution would be impossible without this web of connectivity. Teleology exists on the information and spiritual level in human communities as a constraining force pushing us towards beauty, peace, and harmony and is essential for the continued evolution of mankind. The two teleologies, physical and spiritual, are intertwined. We have seen how Whitehead sees God as the foundation of this physical order and as a spiritual being, one who feels our sorrows and is joyful in our victories.

This viewpoint is not what is known as "Intelligent Design." Intelligent Design assumes that evolutionary states are too complex to be understood by natural systems. Instead, we are claiming the natural laws of mutations fully explain evolution scientifically; however, the physical processes are associated with a mental, spiritual, or information pole, which if considered, offers a truer picture of the outcome of evolution. The spiritual information aspect is complimentary to the physical laws of evolution. Complexity arises naturally from the physical laws because the combination of information and survival demands better information and this ultimately leads to self-knowledgeable beings that can coordinate and cooperate with one another. Thus, from this perspective we see the complexity of the origin of consciousness, reasoning, and language acquisition. While matter and evolution may never be entirely clarified, as Du Bois-Reymond asserted, even if we do eventually find the final physical spark necessary to get to the consciousness of man, we would not diminish man because spirit is beyond physical interpretation and has been in the nature of the world from the beginning.

As to free will, while not provable, all of us are interconnected, and our freedom is often minimal but our human spirit allows us to make choices, to feel guilt, to know love, and to hate evil. Despite our constraints and potential for incorrect choices, all of these possibilities do exist. Our teleology is process through time imbued with intelligence and is consistent with the very substrate of the universe, an intelligent God who allows for our individuality and our spiritual existence, however transient it may be. Whitehead understood the notion of process as a fundamental reality of existence, and the essence of his understanding based on creativity, the eternal forms, and God serves as our best intellectual evidence concerning our world and our freedom.

We have seen tremendous progress in the physical, biological, and medical sciences in the past nearly 150 years; however, on the moral front we have seen World War I, the war to end all wars, with forty million casualties worldwide and about seventeen million deaths. As the technology improved further, World War II with its brutal Nazi regime, the holocaust, and the horrible devastation of civilians at Hiroshima and Nagasaki resulted in eighty million deaths worldwide. With further improvements in technology, smaller wars have continued, and we sit on the brink of mass destruction with our world clinging to nuclear and biological weapons, which can be delivered in seconds around the world.

However, the years since the Second World War have been generally more peaceful than the years from Emil's speech up to 1945. Evil exists and as mentioned previously, all religious beliefs are "shipwrecked on the problem of evil."[1] The God or moral lure of Whitehead's Process Philosophy is one who is against evil but in addition to comforting us, he can guide us in our work against evil and for justice and peace. We need to stand up to those who see the riddles as justification for one race or people as superior to another based on false philosophies, arising out of the distortion of true scientific evolution, where the purpose of man distorts to subjugate, destroy, or enslave other races or religions. Fear, ignorance, and greed are the common denominators that feed such groups. The second tier riddles provide focus for the many practical problems that we have discussed and could help us to create a just and harmonious world.

Quoting Whitehead another time: "The present type of order in the world has arisen from an unimaginable past, and it will find its grave in an unimaginable future. There remain the inexhaustible realm of abstract forms, and creativity, with its shifting character ever determined afresh by its own creatures, and God, upon whose wisdom all forms of order depend."[2]

NOTES

1. Whitehead, Alfred N., 1926, *Religion*, 64.
2. Whitehead, Alfred N., 1926, 142.

Part II

TWO THEOLOGIES FOR THE SEVEN RIDDLES OF THE UNIVERSE

Chapter 11

What is Religion/Theology?

As Whitehead points out in *Religion in the Making* there's no one clear definition of religion. According to Webster religion is "Relating to or manifesting faithful devotion to an acknowledged ultimate reality or deity." Whitehead elucidates the importance of the individual in religion rather than the religious group: "But all collective emotions leave untouched the awful ultimate fact, which is the human being, consciously alone with itself, for its own sake."[1]

Each of us becomes aware of the mystery of the world and asks about the why of our existence. How we answer this question determines our faith and our character. Faith is not limited to religion, for faith, even in science, rests on fundamental postulates not deductible from reason. As George Galloway says: "The difference between theology and religious philosophy is one of degree only; the one lays greater stress on faith, the other on reason; but reason cannot work without faith and faith has its proper ally in reason."[2]

Usually our parents and community help to give us answers to our questions about faith but we constantly reassess these questions as our experience and knowledge grows. The complexity of various backgrounds and cultures leads to a multitude of beliefs and faiths. Whitehead says that: "Religion is the art and theory of the internal life of man, so far as it depends on the man himself and on what is permanent in the nature of things" and "Religion is what the individual does with his own solitariness."[3] Both Whitehead and DeWitt Hyde see the importance of merging our values with the values of others. DeWitt Hyde called his book *Social Theology* because:

"... the Christianity of Christ and his disciples was preeminently a social movement ... we no longer treat man as capable of isolation."[4] Also, "... the adjective 'social' serves to call attention to the shifting of emphasis from the abstract and formal relation of the isolated individual to an external Ruler, over to man's, concrete and essential relations to the Divine Life manifested in nature, history, and human society."[5]

Emotion must be present during a religious experience yet consistency with reason is also essential since it corrects selfish and nonsensical notions. On the other hand, over-codification of dogma leads often to an anti-religious overzealous desire to remove heresy from the ranks of the members. Religion unlike pure science deals with both short and long-term values, purpose, and consequently morality. Can ethics and morality be completely separated from religion? Nietzsche and many non-theist humanists said yes it could be and should be. Doing so removes the connection of long-term value from the short-term one. In the end without the connection between morality and religion one loses some justification for pursuing a meaningful moral life. Without the long-term picture hope can turn to despair and faith can be replaced by a selfish pragmatism. On the other hand, humanists and atheists often have, like most people, an innate sense of guilt about hurtful actions, empathy, and sacrifice even as they dissociate morality from religion. The relationship between character and beliefs is complex.

Art plays a role in religion in that it also reveals a higher purpose in life. Whether it's the famous paintings of Michelangelo's, the Gregorian chants or Ave Maria, art can take one to an emotional state that lifts the soul to a higher place. A quiet early morning walk in a beautiful garden or in the woods also can stir one to sense the mystery and the finer aspects of our limited existence. Understanding the complexities and workings of scientific theories like quantum mechanics or the phenomenal workings of human physiology can stir the soul as much as peering at a starry night sky since in all we recognize the beauty and harmony of the world's design.

There is also no agreement on what constitutes a true religion and a given religion need not necessarily be good but can, as history clearly shows, be evil. For example, the Greeks had a practice of offering two human victims at the Festival of Thargelia in order to restore their relationship with the deity. Religion has been an important element in our civilization's progress especially through the development of moral order; however, it also has been the basis for discrimination, bigotry, and horrific deeds such as mentioned above.

Both science and art have conflicted with religion and this conflict will be discussed further in another chapter. However, in the case of science, new developments can be seen by religious institutions as conflicting with their dogma and they are often unwilling, at least initially, to change their dogmas. The dogma of an earth-centered universe was fought for and eventually was relinquished because the religious institutions finally realized that it did not destroy religion and maybe even strengthened it. Evolution is a theory where conflict still exists when in reality; scientific evolution does not diminish religion if it is viewed from a more global philosophical perspective. Religious institutions have banned artistic books, movies, and video games as a way of avoiding lewd or violent material but such attempts at censorship often work counter to the goal of encouraging followers to consider the concerns about such works.

Scientists often overreach in trying to apply their knowledge to spiritual and moral questions that are not really in their realm. Thus, both sides need to be bold enough to realize their limitations.

Our faith in our overall progress as a spiritual and moral people, through the realization of an ultimate good, is a faith that propels each new generation or degenerates into insincerity and despair. Religion is a means of coming to terms with the reality and mystery of our existence in a way that appreciates the gifts of our existence and credits these to the guiding spiritual power who through our reflection and prayer helps us come to terms with the sadness and evil which exists in the world. This force gives us faith in the overall journey; hope in progress against evil and in addition, takes us beyond ourselves and guides us to a deeply felt love, empathy, and charity to our family and fellow travelers.

Whitehead and DeWitt Hyde give us a rational understanding of deity and guide rails for valid religious beliefs, which we will explore, but first, we will look at both of their lives and works.

NOTES

1. Whitehead, Alfred N., *Religion*, 1926, 7.
2. Galloway, George, *Philosophy*, 1920, 14.
3. Whitehead, Alfred N., 1926, 7.
4. DeWiitt Hyde, William, *Social Theology*, 1910, 2.
5. DeWiitt Hyde, William, 1910, 4.

Chapter 12

Alfred North Whitehead
Life and Works Part 2

Alfred North Whitehead delivered four lectures in King's Chapel, Boston during February 1926. His purpose was to show that our understanding of the world requires recognition of certain "*permanent elements*" without which no order and no changing world could exist.[1]

On the ninth of that month, the teaching of the theory of evolution was forbidden in the Atlanta, Georgia school system. Walt Disney Studios began operation on the eighth and Franco became Spain's youngest general on the twenty-fifth. The King's Chapel goes back to 1688 and still exists today on the Freedom Trail. Since it was a loyalist's church, the members mostly fled to England during the revolution. Subsequently the Chapel came under the control of a Unitarian group. It has a rich history of famous sermons.

Having discussed some aspects of Whitehead's life in the previous section, we will here examine other aspects of his life and examine his works beyond *Religion in the Making*.

On December 16 in 1890 Whitehead married Evelyn Wade in London. She was five years younger than Alfred, of Irish descent, but born and raised in France. She was a very energetic and intelligent woman who supported Alfred immensely. They had three children, two sons and a daughter; the son, Eric Alfred Whitehead, was killed in World War I while flying on a patrol in France in 1918. Eric had wanted to enlist but Evelyn saw to it that he was commissioned on entry. Eric's loss had a profound effect on Alfred and his family and it took years for them to accept his death.

Gaining insight into his personal life is difficult since he had all of his personal papers destroyed after his death. In his two-volume work entitled *Alfred North Whitehead: The Man and his Work*, Victor Lowe describes how little personal information was available.[2] Another source of such information is a book, *Dialogues of Alfred North Whitehead,* written by a former student, Lucien Price, who attended the weekly gatherings that Whitehead had in his home with students and colleagues. Some interesting tidbits come up which often correspond with the turbulent times they lived through. They also reflect upon Whitehead's love of communication and his and Evelyn's genuine humanity. Some simple examples beyond the serious ones include: Alfred: "Is it that nothing, no experience good or bad, no belief, no cause, is, in itself, momentous enough to monopolize the whole of life to the exclusion of laughter? Laughter is a reminder that our theories are attempts to make existence intelligible, but necessarily only an attempt, and does not the irrational, the instinctive burst in to keep the balance true by laughter?[3]

Evelyn: "Dogs are far more moral than most human beings; they are more self-effacing and more self-sacrificing. Watch a dog try to help someone he loves; the beast puts us to shame."[4]

SCIENCE AND THE MODERN WORLD

In 1925 Whitehead published the book, *Science in the Modern World,* which was a compilation of a series of lectures given in the United States and served as the basis of his later metaphysical work. He saw the rise of modern science as the emphasis on "irreducible and stubborn facts" combined with abstract theoretical knowledge and an inherent belief in the order of nature. Whitehead analyses abstract concepts which are often assumed in science and shows how their limitations create the opportunity for more comprehensive and accurate theories. Whitehead refers to what he calls the "fallacy of misplaced concreteness" which occurs, for example, when one assumes an abstract infinitesimal point locates an object. If one assumes an infinitesimal point represents an atom in the atomic theory of gases, it is a good approximation; however, it actually has a small size and this needs to be accounted for in a more accurate theory. The implication of relativity and quantum theory is presented.

Whitehead recognizes how science and culture have interacted and he lays the foundation for his later work on Process Philosophy and Theology. On fundamental beliefs and scientific theories, which are part of the spirit of man, he says: "It (philosophy) builds cathedrals before the workmen have moved a stone, and it destroys them before the elements have worn down their arches. It is the architect of the buildings of the spirit, and it is also their solvent: and the spiritual precedes the material".[5] He points out the importance that science would necessarily play in the future and safety of any society: "It is the business of the future to be dangerous; and it is among the merits of science that it equips the future for its duties."[6] Concerning religion's future, he states: "Religion will not regain its old power until it can face change in the same spirit as does science. Its principles may be eternal, but the expression of those principles requires continual development."[7] On the origins of modern science: "Faith in the possibility of science, generated antecedently to the development of modern scientific theory, is an unconscious derivative from medieval theology."[8]

PROCESS AND REALITY

His most famous book, *Process and Reality*, which lays out the fundamentals of process theory, was first presented in the 1927–1928 session of the Gifford lectures at the University of Edinburgh. The prestigious Gifford Lectureships were established by Adam Lord Gifford (1820–1887), a senator of the College of Justice in Scotland. Lecturers since 1888 have also included Freeman Dyson, William James, and Noam Chomsky. The purposes of the lectures are to "promote and diffuse the study of Natural Theology in the widest sense of the term—in other words, the knowledge of God". In the beginning of his book he lays out his goal which is: "to frame a coherent, logical, necessary system of general ideas in terms of which every element of our experience can be interpreted." His basis of analysis starts with change or process as a fundamental starting point for such interpretation. Whitehead defined a completely new set of vocabulary to use in his construction, which recognizes the relatedness of everything in the universe: "It is presupposed that no entity can be conceived in complete abstraction from the system of the universe, and that it is the business of speculative philosophy to exhibit this truth. This character is its coherence."[9]

Whitehead described the great difficulty that occurs in trying to identify the underlying metaphysical principles which characterize the universe:

"Philosophers can never hope finally to formulate these metaphysical first principles. Weakness of insight and deficiencies in language stand in the way inexorably. Words and phrases must be stretched towards a generality foreign to their ordinary usage; and however such elements of language be stabilized as technicalities, they remain metaphors mutely appealing for an imaginative leap."[10]

Overall, the book is difficult to read, especially the first time going through it, yet it is a masterpiece of construction and is possibly the most novel, comprehensive, and far-reaching philosophical study ever devised.

Aims of Education

His book, *Aims of Education and other Essays,* was published by Macmillan in 1929. He had in 1916 given a talk as his Presidential Address to the Mathematical Society called *Aims of Education–A plea for Reform,* which became a part of a book published in 1917 called *The Organization of Thought Educational and Scientific.* Some of the ideas in these earlier works found their way into *Aims of Education and other Essays.* From the beginning of the Aims book:

> "Culture is activity of thought, and receptiveness to beauty and humane feeling. Scraps of information have nothing to do with it. A merely well-informed man is the most useless bore on God's earth. What we should aim at producing is men who possess both culture and expert knowledge in some special direction. Their expert knowledge will give them the ground to start from, and their culture will lead them as deep as philosophy and as high as art."[11]

The first line is very powerful and unfortunately even higher education has moved further and further away from the humanities, from culture and towards jumping into the practicalities of employment. Yet without the activity of thought and receptiveness to beauty and human feeling, what kind of education do we get? To be an expert in any area once out of schooling requires a significant number of dedicated hours spent each week, thus if culture is not challenged during college, then it will be more difficult to achieve in a profession.

> "Education with inert ideas is not only useless: it is, above all things, harmful - Corruptio optimi, pessima. Except at rare intervals of intellectual ferment, education in the past has been radically infected with inert ideas. That is the reason why uneducated clever women, who have seen much of the world, are in middle life so much the most cultured part of the community. They have been saved from this horrible burden of inert ideas. Every intellectual revolution which has ever stirred humanity into greatness has been a passionate protest against inert ideas. Then, alas, with pathetic ignorance of human psychology, it has proceeded by some educational scheme to bind humanity afresh with inert ideas of its own fashioning."[12]

It is ironic how the last line above shows how ingrained are inert ideas in teaching and how unfortunately simple it is for the teacher to convey them. Whitehead also disliked external standardized exams because they fail to take into account the delicate nature of the many variables upon which successful accomplishment depends.

Students become teachers and as a teacher one has to have a passion to teach where each child is understood, respected, and treated fairly. Teachers need the support of administrators and parents to be creative and flexible. Large classes and too many students can lead to a degradation of the teaching process.

Whitehead understood the importance of imagination in learning and in creating a new world. Where would we be without leaping beyond the present world to a better one in all fields? For example, an imaginative leap combined with hard work took the Wright brothers out of their bicycle shop and off the ground.

PROCESS THEOLOGY–DEVELOPMENTS
SINCE WHITEHEAD

Besides Whitehead, Charles Hartshorne, John Cobb, and David Ray Griffin contributed to the development of Process Theology. As in process philosophy, process theology places greater emphasis on becoming rather than being, and the structure is combined with Judeo-Christian values.[13] Pierre Teilhard de Chardin's works emphasized human physical and spiritual evolution from the alpha towards the omega of godliness and in that sense can be incorporated into the Process Theology category; however, his approach was not philosophically as rigorous and all- encompassing as Whitehead's. It should be pointed out that Chardin, a Jesuit Priest, received significant resistance from the Catholic Church at the time of his writing but has recently, along with Whitehead and Process Theology, been embraced by a fellow Jesuit, Pope Francis. Besides numerous Christian theologians, some Jewish theologians have also embraced the framework of Process Theology.[14]

Liberation Theology is an outgrowth of Process Theology where emphasis on God's nature reveals liberation of the oppressed. Whitehead's God is persuasive, not coercive, and does not embrace the status quo but ever drawing us to a better future. God is not a distant, remote God but rather one who shares in our suffering and our joy and is pulling for the oppressed.[15]

NOTES

1. Whitehead, Alfred N., *Religion*, 1926.
2. Lowe, Victor, *Whitehead Biography*, 2002.
3. Price, Lucien, *Dialogues*, 1954, 55.
4. Price, Lucien, 1954, 190.
5. Whitehead, Alfred N., *Science*, 1929, Preface.

6. Whitehead, Alfred N., *Science*, 1929, 207.
7. Whitehead, Alfred N., *Science*, 1929, 189.
8. Whitehead, Alfred N., *Science*, 1929, 13.
9. Whitehead, Alfred N., *Process*, 1929, 5.
10. Whitehead, Alfred N., *Process*, 1929, 6.
11. Whitehead, Alfred N., *Aims*, 1929, 1.
12. Whitehead, Alfred N., *Aims*, 1929, 99.
13. Griffin, David R., *Reenchantment*, 2001.
14. Teilhard de Chardin, Pierre, *Phenomenon*, 2018.
15. Floyd, Stacy M. et al., Theologies, 2010.

Chapter 13

William DeWitt Hyde

His Life and Works

William DeWitt Hyde was born just before the Civil War in Winchendon, Massachusetts on September 23, 1858. Life expectancy at birth was at that time thirty-eight for men and forty-one for women. His father, Joel, and grandfather, Joe, half farmers and half industrialists, were engaged in making wooden products. His mother was Eliza DeWitt. Her religious and intellectual interests were pursued with an enthusiasm for learning and with strong social inclinations. Their first child, Edward Francis, unfortunately died a few months after birth from diphtheria. A few years later Eliza gave birth to William; however, unfortunately six weeks later his mother passed away at the age of thirty. William was then raised by his nurse who had attended to Eliza during both births. After a few more years, his father, Joel, remarried. William's new stepmother, Catherine Doyle, brought to him discipline hitherto unknown.

When William was eight years old his father passed away at the age of forty-six, leaving the boy with a few thousand dollars but also leaving his care as a problem for the surviving relatives. The stepmother did not wish to keep him, his grandmother had died two months before his father and his grandfather was almost eighty.

Finally, his father's sister, Eliza, came forward with an offer to care for him. Eliza lived with her husband in a scenic home in Keene, New Hampshire yet her husband was a very tough disciplinarian and William was very unhappy. Meanwhile, John Hyde, a cousin of the boy's father, heard about William's distress and at the age of eleven, William joined John and Sarah Hyde's family. William eventually left school and went to work for the Hamilton Woolen Company. While William was an excellent and reliable worker, his Aunt Sarah wanted a liberal education for the boy. With his keen mind, Sarah helped him to achieve admission to Phillips Exeter Academy.

William excelled and was happy during his years at Exeter and was so talented that he was admitted to Harvard University. He started classes at Harvard University in the fall of 1875. At that time about one-fourth of the class came from Boston while about forty percent lived outside of Massachusetts, scattered over seventeen states and several foreign countries. Three-quarters of the graduating class of Exeter went to Harvard. He graduated with honors from Harvard. According to Dr. Burnett, his biographer, one particular classmate had retained the following impression of him as a senior: "He became rather a marked man in respect to reasoning powers and general force of character. I should say, at the end of his senior year, he showed a maturity which few men ever attain, and hardly any until they have been out of college for a number of years."[1] He was chosen as commencement speaker for the graduation and the title of his speech was *"The Modern Idolatry of Culture."* Dr Burnett gave the following excerpt from the speech:

"We hear little nowadays of inspiration in speech and writing and less of obligation in study and literary work. We forget that all true growth is from within, and seek to extend our being by additions from without. This culture seeks not to feel, but rather to see what feeling is, speculate about its nature and add this knowledge to its other acquisitions. Self is made a false center around which everything else revolves."[2]

While modern culture is denounced by each generation, I believe he would be flabbergasted to see so many of us buried in our cell phones with quick access to the outside world of information, news, sports, movies, and music.

For one year, he matriculated as a graduate student at Union Theological Seminary in New York. He then transferred to Andover Seminary back in New England. William changed because he felt that he was not obtaining the courses on modern philosophical inquiry available at Union Seminary. While at Andover, he met a wonderful young woman, Prudence Phillips, with whom he fell in love. This led to an engagement and marriage within two years. According to Dr. Burnett, "Ms. Phillips was the daughter of a grain merchant of New York City, had lost her mother, and from the age of seven lived with her grandparents on a farm south of the center of Southbridge." Dr Burnett gives an excerpt of a letter that he wrote to her:

"You speak of having passed from a mood of sad disbelief in the world to one of happy trust. Is not the better way—the truer way in consideration of the facts, to be in both all the time? That is to say: there is a Devil and there is a God; and the world of human hearts is divided between the two. With reference to those hearts under the former sway our sadness and our unbelief can never be too deep. It must not be forgotten when a warmer current happens for the moment to strike our individual course. With reference to the latter class, our joy and trust can never be too great—that must not be lost when the sky over our individual head grows cloudy. And we must be prepared to keep this dual faith unshaken, when the particular individuals whom we most distrusted or most loved prove just the opposite of what we had supposed."[3]

During the summer of 1883 he wrote an article which was published in the *New Englander Magazine* in the September edition entitled the *"Metaphysical Basis of Belief in God"*, a part of which is again quoted by Dr. Burnett:

"The metaphysical basis of belief in God is found in the fact that the individual consciousness is a two-fold unity of a universal and a particular element. . . . God is not an imaginary being, a product of thought, but a Being without whose existence, thought itself could not exist in its several modes actually operative in the life of every man."[4]

In 1883 William, newly engaged to Miss Phillips, was hired as a pastor for the Born Street Congregational Church of Paterson, New Jersey. The home at 199 Godwin Street did not have to wait long for its new family. On November 6 a quiet wedding took place in Washington, New York. Besides his pastor role, he also had time for his second metaphysical paper on consciousness published in *the New Englander*:

"Spiritual life that is not love is unthinkable. . . . Even God himself, if he ceased to love any creature with whom he was in conscious relation, would cease to be. Eternal life consists in persistent devotion to the common good, i.e., the good of all fellow-creatures; eternal death is persistent devotion to private good, i.e., the gratifying of purely selfish impulses. Infants are not yet endowed with the power and joy of spiritual life. . . . Their only hope . . . is that either here or elsewhere they may develop into spiritual life."[5]

With sad irony on October 10, twins were born; however, by October 24 both had died. The article was published in the November issue.

Because of his intellectual powers, his peers believed he should be hired in an academic setting. According to Burnett, "Bowdoin College had a trustee named Egbert C Smyth, the son of a distinguished professor of mathematics in that institution, himself a teacher there for eleven years in various departments who also had been at Andover seminary to teach ecclesiastical history and was now the president of that institution. He and the school offered William a Chair in Philosophy and also the Presidency of the college." Such a dramatic step up shows just how impressive his intelligence and character were.

Before starting his position on that last day of July he read before the *American Institute of Christian Philosophy*, in what was then known as Key East, New Jersey and now is Avon by the Sea. In his presentation, *Ethics and Religion*, which afterwards was published in the proceedings of that society he stated:

> "If philosophy is not itself immediately practical, yet in this intensely practical world it must vindicate its right to be by grappling with the concrete facts and forces of the real world. Of all practical affairs, nothing is more practical than matters of ethics and religion. . . . The miserable and pitiful attempts to rear religious life on transitory excitement, or on elaborate ritual, or schemes of divinity, or dread of future punishment, each have had their brief day and seeming success, and then ceased to be. Ethics alone gives a solid groundwork needed; for it is the science of that self-realization of man of which the union with God given in religion is the consummation."[6]

Dr. Hyde was well received by the students and faculty of Bowdoin College in Brunswick, Maine. He was close to the students and often gave them informal talks at Sunday Chapel. Initially he was considered the boy President. On the 250th anniversary founding of Harvard, he was invited to deliver a lecture at Harvard. He also spoke at the Regents convocation in New York on July 7, 1886. The lecture was titled *Relation of Higher Education to Religion.* He became famous, and there came at least tentative approaches to a remarkable offer, the presidency of the University of California. His first book, *Practical Ethics*, was just coming to press. He turned down that offer and six others to stay at Bowdoin. The offer from the University of California arrived after the publication of his widely discussed article on "*Impending Paganism*". He sought advice in terms of making this important decision; however, in the end he sent the following letter on September 8, 1894 to his friend, Professor Elliot:

> "I thank you for Professor Derby's letter which I enclose. I have sought all the light I could get on both sides; and have declined. I am not afraid of the responsibilities of promotion; but I shall remain here until promotion comes along the particular line in which I can do best. I have declined six other offers at salaries ranging from four to seven thousand dollars within the past six years."[7]

During the years 1905 to 1907 the president was caught in the midst of a controversy regarding a professor who had become deaf and was unable to teach properly. He felt the heavy weight of the tug and pull with the Board of Trustees and by the time it was fully resolved his health had begun to deteriorate. On a campaign to raise $150,000 for the school, he lectured in New

York at an alumni meeting in January 1907. During the talk he fainted, and he showed similar tendencies at home. An examination revealed that heart failure was the cause. In February, he discontinued all college work for the remainder of the year, and abandoned ordinary social life. In June 1907 he was given the six-month leave with permission to extend it to a year.

To the Yale freshmen, in the fall of 1916, within a year of his demise, Hyde said:

"Athletics, society, science, art, history are only so many fractions of life. Neither of them, nor all together, with business, politics, wealth, and love thrown in, can make us see life whole, and lift us to the eternal point of view. That is the province of philosophy: to see real unity underneath seeming diversity; to discover order in apparent chaos; to unveil mind in the disguises of matter; to throw the bridges of rational hypothesis across the chasms of blind unintelligibility—and to do this not in conceited and futile independence, but in all the light the masters of reflection, Plato, Aristotle, Descartes, Spinoza, Kant, Hegel, Royce, Bergson, can lend you. Do you then under some unifying principle ideas, energy, monads, reason, will, the thing that works, the vital impulse, happiness, duty, or self-realization—endeavor to unify the world and give man's life setting in a coherent and intelligible whole? Then you are taking up the philosophic side of your human inheritance, and putting a line of demarcation between you and the brutes."[8]

DeWitt Hyde published a number of books of which his book, *Social Theology*, will be discussed in detail in a future chapter. Here we will review some of his other works.

In *Practical Idealism*, he points out that the natural evils in the world are based on good things which are necessary for our existence. For example, when one falls and is injured from the effect of gravity, the gravity is a necessary condition for us. So natural evils must be recognized and steps should be taken to avoid the bad consequences of this force. Evil resulting from the heart of men or women is more difficult and needs to be addressed through pity for the sinner and an effort to deliver him from his sin. If we are the sinners, we need to repent and reject the sin and in both cases, the grace of God is needed to forgive and move on through our ultimate understanding of his love for us.

A striking illustration of the effectiveness of this book, *Practical Idealism*, was its effect on a young man, a student from China who for some years had brooded with unspeakable sadness upon the burdens and moral failure of human life.[9] He was becoming a confirmed pessimist, when he began reading a copy of Hyde's book. He attributed the book to the beginnings of his optimism and his conversion to Christianity. He then founded a private school known as Nankai Middle School and University, where students were drawn from all parts of China and some western countries. The school after the revolution became government run but still exists today.

Practical Ethics covers all the virtues and fundamental aspects of ethical behavior. Examples of his writing are plain ethical concepts:

> "Truth is fidelity to fact; it plants itself upon reality; and hence it speaks with authority. The truthful man is one whom we can depend upon. His word is as good as his bond."[10] "Truth is often opposed to sacred traditions, inherited prejudices, popular beliefs, and vested interests." "Exposing the truth often exposes one to abuse and even to loss on one's life."[11] "Anxiety sacrifices the present to the future." "Procrastination sacrifices the future to the present."[12] "Courage (is) to do right when everyone around us is doing wrong; courage to say 'No' when everyone is trying to make us say 'Yes'."[13] "The brave man plants himself on the eternal foundations of truth and justice, and bids defiance to all the forces that would drive him from it."[14]

While we make *Social Theology* the focus of this book, his most popular book has been *The Five Great Philosophies of Life.* It is an excellent book for an introductory university philosophy course. He concentrates on Epicurean, Stoic, Plato-Socratic, Aristotelian, and Christian philosophies of how to live your life. Some excerpts are: Quoting DeWitt Hyde on Epicurus regarding overdoing self-sacrifice: "But one whose bodily vigor and mental health are undermined by self-sacrifice carried too far, in the first place becomes to those around a cause of depression, and in the second place renders himself incapable, or less capable, of actively furthering their welfare."[15]

On the Stoics from Epictetus: "If I feel humiliated and stung by it, it is because I am weak and foolish enough to stake my estimate of myself, and my consequent happiness, upon what somebody who does not know me says about me, rather than on what I, who know myself better than anybody else, actually think."[16]

HYDE QUOTING EPICTETUS

> "Remember, then, that if you attribute freedom to things by nature dependent, and seek for your own that which is really controlled by others, you will be hindered, you will lament, you will be disturbed, you will find fault both with gods and men. But if you take for your own only that which is your own, and view what belongs to others just as it really is, then no one will ever compel you, no one will restrict you; you will find fault with no one, you will accuse no one,

you will do nothing against your will; no one will hurt you, you will not have an enemy, nor will you suffer any harm."[17]

ON PLATO

"The reason why the life of a righteous man is happier than the life of an unrighteous man is that it has 'a greater share in pure existence as a more real being.'"[18] ". . . Men become lovers of trade and of money, and they honor and reverence the rich man and make a ruler of him, and dishonor the poor man." "The evils of this oligarchical rule, he says, are illustrated by considering the nature of the qualification for office and influence. Just think what would happen if the pilots were to be chosen according to their property, and a poor man refused permission to steer, even though he was the better pilot? The other defect is the inevitable division; such a state is not one but two states . . . (Plato)"[19] "The most righteous man is also the happiest, and this is he who is the most royal master of himself; the worst and most unrighteous man is also the most miserable; this is he who is also the greatest tyrant of himself and the most complete slave."[20]

ON ARISTOTLE

Plato's eternal forms and God inspire the concept of righteousness and Aristotle examines, like the scientist in him, what requirements are necessary to have a good and happy life. He is not against the safety and pleasures of Epicurus nor the fortitude of the stoic yet he sees that the goals we set up for ourselves demand knowledge and reason but also temperance and wisdom. One needs justification for our desires from a big picture of our overall goals. The methods used to accomplish our goals must be just. What we need also is courage to endure some hardship to achieve our goals. Thus, pain and suffering are not to be avoided at all costs like the Epicureans and not to be just accepted as the Stoics. Happiness then consists of living life with just ways of desiring noble goals and requires knowledge, temperance, and wisdom. DeWitt Hyde sums up Aristotle's approach: "A man is what he does. He can do nothing except what he first sees as an unaccomplished idea, and then bends all his energies to accomplish. In working out his ideas and making them real, he at the same time works out his own powers, and becomes a living force, a working will in the world."[21] People's abilities vary and sometimes people are incapacitated, yet they can still give and receive love. With that said we move on to the fifth philosophy of life considered as a philosophy, not as religion.

ON CHRISTIANITY

Plato and Aristotle went part of the way in terms of defining a philosophy of life; however, DeWitt Hyde sees Christian philosophy as the fifth and more complete vision: "Not until the city-state of Plato and Aristotle is widened to include the humblest man, the lowliest woman, the most defenseless little child, does their doctrine become final and universal."[22] Christ taught by example, by parables and propositions. Jesus requires that "our lives shall detract nothing from and add something to the glory of God and the welfare of man."[23] The Christian philosophy of life is defined by love: "He translated into the actual fact of a community united in Love." . . . He "taught us to make every human interest we touch as precious as our own."[24]

After 1916, William's health declined and he passed away at the end of June 1917 at the age of fifty-eight. Dr. Burnett eloquently describes the scene at the burial of this extraordinary man on July 2, 1917:

> "There were no carriages in the procession to the cemetery that lies, close hemmed by the sentinel pines, just beyond the campus. Mrs. Hyde and her son walked with the others—friends and neighbors, men of high station, trustees and overseers, faculty, alumni and students—along the scant quarter-mile of elm-shaded road, past Memorial Hall and old Massachusetts and past the big yellow house in whose shady grounds the tired and stricken teacher had strolled less than a week before. . . . After Mr. Ashby had read the committal service, in a flower-bordered grave in the shade of a little tree of thick foliage we left the sleeping teacher."[25]

NOTES

1. Burnett, Charles Theodore, *Hyde of Bowdoin*, 1931, 50.
2. Burnett, Charles Theodore, 1931, 51.
3. Burnett, Charles Theodore, 1931, 83.
4. Burnett, Charles Theodore, 1931, 85.
5. Burnett, Charles Theodore, 1931, 89.
6. Burnett, Charles Theodore, 1931, 99–101.
7. Burnett, Charles Theodore, 1931, 140–141.
8. Burnett, Charles Theodore, 1931, 275–276.
9. DeWitt Hyde, William, *Practical Idealism*, 1899.
10. DeWitt Hyde, William, *Practical Ethics*, 1892, 50.
11. DeWitt Hyde, William, 1892, 52.
12. DeWitt Hyde, William, 1892, 58.
13. DeWitt Hyde, William, 1892, 66.
14. DeWitt Hyde, William, 1892, 67.

15. DeWitt Hyde, William, *Five Great Philosophies*, 1924, 15.
16. DeWitt Hyde, William, 1924, 71.
17. DeWitt Hyde, William, 1924, 71.
18. DeWitt Hyde, William, 1924, 145.
19. DeWitt Hyde, William, 1924, 136.
20. DeWitt Hyde, William, 1924, 145.
21. DeWitt Hyde, William, 1924, 178.
22. DeWitt Hyde, William, 1924, 198.
23. DeWitt Hyde, William, 1924, 204.
24. DeWitt Hyde, William, 1924, 204.
25. Burnett, Charles Theodore, 1931, 341.

Chapter 14

Process Theology

Further Analysis

As a mathematician and a scientist, Whitehead wanted to develop a fundamental structure to understand our universe. In addition, as mentioned previously, he was a classical scholar and nurtured in historical religious experience. He wanted any universal theory to be consistent with scientific logical verification and yet one that addresses ethics, poetry, literature, art, and religious notions.

He believed that a theory about our universe had to fundamentally address change or process inherent in the universe. Like Heraclitus who said that, "You can never step into the same river twice," Whitehead saw change as fundamental to our existence.

In science, stating basic definitions and postulates is essential in any theory. For example, in quantum mechanics the Wavefunction Postulate assumes that for any physical system the wavefunction determines everything known about the system. Some assumptions are slightly incorrect and corrections to them can be added when needed.

In order to explain process, Whitehead invoked postulates or assumptions similar to those used in science. Process must be grounded in elements that are not changing since there must be some consistency, even as change occurs, otherwise process would be totally chaotic.

Whitehead defines one tiny element of Process as an actual entity. It is not a fixed instant of time or fixed interval of space yet almost an infinitesimal drop of experience. The three postulated concepts chosen as a necessary basis for Process Theory include Creativity, the Eternal Forms, and God. The act of transitioning from one actual entity to the next is called Creativity. But Creativity alone without constraints would be chaotic. This is similar to a movie projector, the creativity, driving the reel. If each frame in the film is all in order then a movie is formed; however, if randomly disordered it would be gibberish.

Our time independent Platonic abstract notions of various forms of being are called the eternal forms and they allow us to characterize actual entities. They can describe real or imaginary objects. They conjoin with creativity and God in the process of actual entities. The final element needed to characterize process is God. He provides the constraints on the physical laws that govern matter and the lure for mankind towards the moral laws and spiritual harmony. Without him process would have no meaning.

Let us look at the reasonableness of these postulates and then ask if they are sufficient.

First, is it justifiable to say that abstract concepts can explain process in physics and chemistry? Yes, since physics and chemistry, elucidated with mathematics, often yield quantitative predictive results about our physical world through the abstract notions and equations that govern them. Whether it is the orbits of satellites or the atomic spectrum of atoms and molecules, predictive power is achievable. Can abstract and quantitative concepts help understand process in areas other than the physical sciences, which includes human emotion, music, art, and religion? Is this at least a reasonable assumption? Overall yes, causality in these realms exists; however, they are much more complex than inanimate force models and interpretations vary somewhat depending on subjective notions. The subjectivity arises in accordance with the existence of several possible interpretations and with the individual's propensity for weighing one as most important based on previous experience. Applying Bayes' Theorem to these cases can give some credence as to a best or most probable interpretation.[1] Whitehead, however, points out that for some situations a poet or an artist or just a mother can sometimes capture keen insights into notions not fully obtainable by rational arguments. Whitehead states: "Yet mothers can ponder many things in their hearts which their lips cannot express. These many things, which are thus known, constitute the ultimate religious evidence, beyond which there is no appeal."[2]

Like any problem it is often helpful to break it up into smaller pieces and thus each moment in process can be captured as an actual entity and each actual entity is continually transformed into a new actual entity, which is a reasonable assumption. The new actual entity depends on the previous one which in turn depends on its previous one, etc. In actuality then the current actual entity depends even on the moment of the origin of our universe in The Big Bang. We know from physics that such time dependent analysis works from some starting point where the laws exist yet at the origin of The Big Bang the laws falter. In physics the time evolution can fully be described only when the interval between steps is infinitesimally small. Whitehead's concept of an actual entity is vague or flexible depending on how you look at it. How much is the short time interval and what is the range throughout influential space?

Is the notion of Creativity as a fundamental postulate reasonable? Creativity is transformation in general distinct from meaningful transformation. Whitehead says change is a reality of our universe but change can be disordered and thus Creativity includes that possibility. It takes information and intelligence to create order. In the physics of motion the fundamental equations of classical or quantum theory govern each actual occasion; however, in quantum theory the occasions can only be described in a probabilistic sense.

Each actual entity has a physical and mental pole. The amount of mental pole depends upon the measure of novelty in an event. This concept is a major departure from traditional ideas and yet in the actual occasion framework, it makes sense because while a given occasion may have directly no significant novelty, the universal environment of the actual occasion is imbued with novelty.

Let us look at the second component, namely the Eternal Forms. We have been blessed with this ability to abstract universal forms both real and imaginary, store them in memory, and verbalize them. The eternal forms are our connection to our social reality. They are non-physical and are information and knowledge. They are the basis for logical constructs. They are the crucible of our imagination and art. The forms of existent objects and concepts are constrained somewhat by the natural physical laws. With foresight of possibilities, purpose to action, and a consideration of values, such action brings out novelty. Creativity conjoined with God steers the potential eternal forms towards aesthetic beauty and assumes a complex coordination in creating a new actual entity. In Whitehead's theory creativity becomes a coequal with God.

The forms are the abstract collection of what is and what is conceivable. Plato was fascinated with forms as the abstraction of the essence of something which was pure and existed beyond the confines of space and time. He also believed that our world was always a poor imitation of the ideal forms. For example, justice as an eternal form is never fully met in the real world. Our finite world is just a shadow of the truths manifested in the eternal forms. Plato realized the human mind's ability to abstract these forms was a gift of the spirit from "beyond the heavens".

Whitehead believed that progress in both science and religion: "is mainly a progress in the framing of concepts."[3]

One particular abstraction which has been around since the beginning of mankind is some notion of God or the ultimate being who is in some way responsible for our world and is reflected in our ability to grasp eternal forms. God, throughout the ages, is considered invisible, beyond finite and yet knowable, at least in the hearts of most men and women. The reason to invoke God as the third fundamental postulate is that creativity and the eternal forms alone cannot allow for ordered aesthetic process. God is the intelligence of the universe who constrains creativity with physical and spiritual laws.

Once we have established the necessity of God, the question of his nature arises. If one has an intelligent God, then one would look for purpose in his relationship to the world. In the case of human social process, God's vision of beauty, justice, and of a harmonious society is the lure or constraint on the human spirit. God possesses the above aesthetic subsets of the ideal eternal forms and draws us to them. Human history, with many bumps in the road, is consistent with attempts to emulate progress in social interactions and to search for truth, harmony, justice, and peace. In investigating the truth in our world, science has brought us to great heights and with applications of the knowledge obtained, we have eliminated many illnesses and diseases and improved transportation and communication. But how does Whitehead's God relate to the individual rather than the vast arc of history?

Digressing a moment, some ask why invoke God when maybe there are trillions of universes, each with different interaction patterns, and we happen to be in this one that has laws consistent with life. First, there is no clear evidence that other universes exist and if they did, then how could you create a theory which explains how the other universes exist without a constraining intelligence? Utilizing Bayes' Theorem, the Oxford philosopher, Richard Swinburne, calculated that, among the known choices, God is probabilistically a much more likely explanation of our ordered universe.[4]

So to answer our earlier question, Whitehead transcends the notion of God being an impersonal force by describing God as the comforter who at the same time suffers with us because his lure is towards harmony, justice, and peace. The basic postulates do not necessarily have to include a personal God directly but not to do so would be in Whitehead's view inconsistent with harmony, peace, justice, and beauty, and when it comes to the individual, inconsistent with the concept of love. As in John 13:34: "A new command I give you. Love one another as I have loved you." Love is the intimate recognition of the value of each soul as he faces his transitory existence in a complex and uncertain world. Man's need for God is reflected back by God's need for man. We live in the spirit, and he is the ultimate manifestation of spirit.

Note that Whitehead tries to avoid questions which are really not logically answerable. He does not ascribe actual creation of the physical universe to God. Instead, he ascribes the physical laws to him and leaves the question of creation alone. Whitehead's God does not exist prior to the universe. He does not want to get into the infinite regression conundrum of then who created God, etc. Furthermore, if God created everything, then God allows evil in the world which is contradictory, in Whitehead's view, to his character. However, traditionalists argue that allowing evil is necessary to allow for individual identities and individual freedom. Whitehead, in *Religion in the Making*, says that because of the evil in the world, possibly his process theory needs additional "formative elements".[5]

What kind of formative element would be necessary? C.S. Lewis in his book, *The Screwtape Letters*, made a good case for how our logic and abstraction can be turned upside down by evil forces to convince people to sin.[6] Whitehead, later in his life, felt that process itself, with the fleeting past that exists only as an abstraction for us, is a source of evil: "The ultimate evil in the temporal world," Whitehead says, "is deeper than any specific evil. It lies in the fact that the past fades, that time is a 'perpetual perishing.'"[7]

Combine this with the freedom that man has to do evil as well as good and the natural evils that exist for an individual in nature and one can conclude that evil has its origin in the creative nature of the universe itself. Who takes responsibility for the world of evil as it is? God is leading us towards harmony, justice, etc. and thus some evil must exist that he clearly recognizes. The world is tainted and the kingdom is good. Whitehead's God is an attempt to have him free of any responsibility for evil since he is only a co-creator with man by allowing mankind the freedom to carve their own destiny while he is only a guide. However, this argument is problematic because once you state that God imposed the physical constraints on matter and energy, this creates an ultimate teleology destined for individuality, freedom, and both natural and human evil. One attempt around this is that God did not make the fleeting temporal process and had only limited choices in constraining Creativity. As philosopher, Thomas E. Hosinski says: ". . . there is nothing God can do to prevent the 'perpetual perishing' inherent in the temporal process." Also, "The possibility of evil goes hand in hand with the possibility of good."[8]

Whitehead's God is not the creator of process and its problems. The world exists, it has individuality and order, but each moment is ephemeral. It has potential evils for individual entities and has given freedom to man to mitigate or worsen evil. This reality can lead to feelings of absurdity regarding human events as described by various existentialist authors.

Beyond the question of evil, Whitehead's God is free of evil and he finally incorporates all temporal actual entities in unification and redemption. According to Whitehead: "The revolts of destructive evil, purely self-regarding, are dismissed into their triviality of merely individual facts; and yet the good they did achieve in individual joy, in individual sorrow, in the introduction of needed contrast, is yet saved by its relation to the completed whole."[9]

He also stated:

"This immortality of the world of action, derived from its transformation in God's nature is beyond our imagination to conceive. The various attempts at description are often shocking and profane. What does haunt our imagination is that the immediate facts of present action pass into permanent significance for the universe. The insistent notion of right and wrong, achievement and failure depends upon this background. Otherwise every activity is merely a passing whiff of insignificance."[10]

NOTES

1. McGrayne, Sharon Bertsch, *The Theory*, 2011.
2. Whitehead, Alfred North, *Religion*, 1926, 55.
3. Whitehead, Alfred North, 1926, 111.
4. Swinburne, Richard, *Theism*, 2016.
5. Whitehead, Alfred North, 1926, 84.
6. Lewis, C.S., *Screwtape Letters*, 2001.
7. Hosinski, Thomas, *Stubborn Fact*, 1998, 216.
8. Hosinski, Thomas, 1998, 217.
9. Whitehead, Alfred North, *Process*, 1929, 340.
10. Johnson, A.H., *Interpretation*, 1961, 265.

Chapter 15

Social Theology

Outlines of Social Theology was first published in 1895 by William DeWitt Hyde by MacMillan Press. His idea was to develop a theology based on the practical social interactions which contour the definition of our individual soul. Fundamentally, without other individuals our behavior loses morality except unto ourselves and without the love and reflection of others, we lose purpose. So, on the one hand, God and the individual have a fundamental, personal, and extraordinary bond; yet it's with our families and fellow travelers that we do God's work. He starts the book with an abstract, theoretical approach to theology but then quickly moves to the social aspects. However, in his understanding of the philosophy he shows great insight. DeWitt Hyde understood, as does Process Philosophy, that external sensory input exists only to the extent it is processed by the mind and interpreted by the mind, but importantly, he recognizes that objective truths about the world are attainable. He sees that we incorporate the outside world through an active intelligence working with the possession of the eternal forms: ". . . an active intelligence which contributes out of its own nature the forms and categories by which it reduces the manifold of sensation to the unity of reason."[1]

As to objective truths, he points to some examples where truth wasn't accepted, first regarding Copernicus: "He is prepared to show that with his doctrine of the revolution of the earth, all other astronomical facts fall into harmony; without this doctrine, all other facts remain in confusion and contradiction."[2] He then asks if ". . . the intelligence by which we interpret the world is simply our intelligence?"[3] His answer is that the physical laws, which have been confirmed and universally accepted, indicate a universal intelligence or God.

On the universal moral laws, which mankind has developed, he points to an Absolute Mind or Universal Will. The example he gives for this is Socrates being told he could live if he renounced his vocation and teaching. Socrates chooses: "Men of Athens, I honor and love you; but I shall obey God rather than you, and while I have life and breath I shall never cease from the practice and teaching of philosophy. For I do believe that there are gods, and in a far higher sense than that in which any of my accusers believe in them."[4] Like Copernicus, he stood up for the truth. Socrates not only defends his moral belief in gods and universal truths being discoverable, but also stands up for his right to free speech, setting the stage for all men and women to discover universal moral truths. "Just as the possibility of error is proof positive of the reality of truth . . . so the consciousness of wrong is the infallible witness of the reality of right, and of its eternal ground in the Universal Will that makes for righteousness."[5]

On an existential level, DeWitt Hyde viewed the external world as constantly changing, but our spirit is always yearning for more than fragile stability that the world at best offers.

"The incapacity of the finite and fleeting world without to satisfy the spirit within, is the half-truth of pessimism and the secret of its charm."[6] He understood the effects of change or process and the wide interconnectedness of our existence:

> "This man upon the street derives his present being from countless generations of men and women who bridged for him the gulf between the savage and the civilized estate; to numberless animal forms which in the struggle for existence won the right of his superior structure to survive; to liberties secured on ancient battlefields and institutions inherited from unremembered days; to parents, friends, teachers, books, influences, ideals . . ."[7]

For DeWitt Hyde the existing proofs (first cause, cosmological, etc.) for the existence of God were false: "As demonstrations of the existence of a Being anterior to creation and external to the world, these proofs are fallacious in method and illusory in result. As expositions of immanent causality and immanent teleology and immanent rationality in nature and in man, they all contain elements of truth."[8] Therefore, he saw the necessity of building metaphysics from an immanent God, as Whitehead would eventually accomplish. He said that Absolute Mind and the Universal Will couldn't be put secondary to nature:

> "It is there of itself. It is presupposed in the facts. It is the source of science and the foundation of morals. Were there no Absolute Mind, there could be no science; were there no Universal Will, there could be no firm basis for morality. Science and morality, however, are real, patent, indisputable facts. Therefore, that without which these facts could not be, must exist."[9]

DeWitt Hyde then wonders about the nature of this God. His argument says that the part cannot be greater than the whole. Namely, since we possess consciousness, reasoning, and personality, then God cannot be less so. God would be expected to far exceed our best abilities in all spiritual elements. DeWitt Hyde claims that God is knowable in the here and now. We see his immanent handiwork in every beautiful sunrise, in a peaceful early morning walk in a garden, in scientific discovery, in a mother's or father's hug or compliment. He described parenthood as the essence of his relationship to us:

"God is our Father, because he is the all-embracing thought which includes each thought and action of every human mind; because he is the holy will which presents the ideal of conduct and the demand of duty to every finite will; because he is the loving heart which finds no human soul alien to itself; because he is the bond which binds things and thoughts together; because he is the unity in which society and individuals find their common ground and from which they derive their mutual obligation; because he is the Spirit in whom we live and move and have our being; who is never far from any one of us, for we are his offspring."[10]

As a Christian, he believed Christ was a perfect example of the abstract notions of divinity manifested in our world. His sonship to God means:

". . . healing of the sick; the comforting of those in sorrow; the relief of the poor; the instruction of the ignorant; the reproof of the wayward; the exposure of the hypocrite; the overthrow of the extortioner; the forgiveness of the penitent; the encouragement of the weak; the succor of the tempted; the emancipation of the prisoner; the solace of mourners at the funeral; the blessing of little children; the provision for the necessities of old age; the imparting of courage to do the work of life and serenity to meet the hour of death; the utterance of truth even when it is most unwelcome; and the doing of duty even at the cost of life itself."[11]

While he made his case for Christianity, he also clarified that Social Theology founded on these principles is consistent with all denominations of major religions of the world. He wanted to ground religion on the best in human virtues (which he felt Christ exemplified), not just abstract philosophical notions. He explained that for generations before rational man, self-interest ruled and where altruism occurred, while it could be emotional, it was mostly instinctual. Rationality combined with emotion allowed control of our natural appetites for our individual and social welfare. Spirit and reason combine in social theology: "Spirit is reason realized in personality. The spiritual life is the universal life; the life determined by reason."[12] "Reason is the common bond that binds mankind together."[13] "Reason bids us treat the moment, not as an isolated self-sufficient thing, but as an element in a larger whole. It bids us rise from the temporal to the eternal point of view. It bids us treat the ideal future as of equal worth with existing present fact."[14]

Social Theology recognizes the strife over men's needs and believes that "strife can be harmonized" when seen from the height of one Universal Will. "To give everybody just what they want is neither possible nor desirable; even after you have come to appreciate what their wants are."[15] On the other hand, DeWitt Hyde points to the Christian basis of Social Theology, namely Matthew 25. The criterion for a right relation with God and the distinction between good and evil is put forth. "I was thirsty, and ye gave me drink; I was a stranger, and you took me in; naked and you clothed me, sick and you visited me. . . . Inasmuch as ye did it unto one of these my brethren, even these least, ye did it unto me."

Sin is acknowledged when we realize our actions were harmful to others and could have been avoided if we had not been so self-interested. Sin can be associated with meanness, dishonesty, bigotry, and hypocrisy. Laws with punishments are ways of governing sinful behavior. Religious laws as well as civil laws can sometimes be overzealous, sinful, and cause harm. Guilt can lead to repentance. If the repentance is sincere, then forgiveness by the injured party can clear the bitterness and pain and affirm the future for both parties. Matthew 5:24. "Leave your gift there before the altar, and go your way. First be reconciled to your brother, and then come and offer your gift." Sin, guilt, repentance, and forgiveness are all realities of our lives independent of belief system but the way we handle the ramifications of their presence varies with our total background and experiences, and if we have a set of fundamental beliefs. DeWitt Hyde believed in a personal God who guides us towards a good and just life. A personal God means communication, and prayer is a mechanism for communication. However, some people pray for the miraculous rather than for guidance. "The attempt to cheat God by using him as a means to the gratification of our private whims and caprices is doubtless futile. God is not mocked."[16]

Prayer brings our suffering, our guilt, our fears, our joy, our successes, and our failings to him so we can apprehend God's mind and values and with that mirrored reflection, we can move forward with faith, hope, and dignity. "Answer to prayer belongs not to the realm of magic and miracle; but lies clearly within the sphere of causality and law."[17] Thanksgiving if truly felt is an element of prayer that recognizes that despite the horrendous evils that can confront us, expressing thanks in prayer reaffirms our finite nature, our small role in a long history of generations, and provides recognition that our ability to grasp the vastness and mystery of the universe is a reflection of an eternal wisdom.

In Christianity, Christ shows compassion and forgiveness. Whether it is the prodigal son or:

"Lord, how many times shall I forgive my brother when he sins against me? Up to seven times?" Matthew 18:21–22. Or "Father, forgive them; for they know not what they do." God teaches the universal lesson of empathy and compassion whenever possible and this allows for reconciliation. DeWitt Hyde said: "This revelation of forgiveness and grace is the central and crowning message of Christianity."[18] He appreciated that grace is the mirror image of love.

A vindictive God without grace would be no god at all. Grace does not mean one is without judgment and corrective of evil. "Then He said to the disciples, 'It is impossible that no offenses should come, but woe to him through whom they do come! It would be better for him if a millstone were hung around his neck, and he were thrown into the sea, than that he should offend one of these little ones'" Luke 17. DeWitt Hyde provided a good example of the lack of grace that can occur even among creative people:

"We know what mean jealousies and petty strifes and bitter animosities such an attitude engenders among poets, painters, preachers, musicians, orators, scientist, and statesman. We know, or ought to know, that nothing but falsehood and folly, hideousness and hate, can ever be the outcome of such an animus. The man who will write lines that shall be remembered, or speak words that men shall heed, or do work that shall endure, must quit trying to be smart. He must care little for the fate of his private, pet hypothesis (as to) who will extend the domains of real science. He should see instead the change from the seeking of selfish satisfaction to the service of truth and beauty, in him who will be scholar and artist."[19]

NOTES

1. DeWitt Hyde, William, *Social Theology*, 1910, 13.
2. DeWitt Hyde, William, 1910, 16.
3. DeWitt Hyde, William, 1910, 13.
4. DeWitt Hyde, William, 1910, 18.
5. DeWitt Hyde, William, 1910, 23.
6. DeWitt Hyde, William, 1910, 8.
7. DeWitt Hyde, William, 1910, 10.
8. DeWitt Hyde, William, 1910, 26.
9. DeWitt Hyde, William, 1910, 29.
10. DeWitt Hyde, William, 1910, 39.
11. DeWitt Hyde, William, 1910, 52.
12. DeWitt Hyde, William, 1910, 78.
13. DeWitt Hyde, William, 1910, 49.

14. DeWitt Hyde, William, 1910, 78.
15. DeWitt Hyde, William, 1910, 81.
16. DeWitt Hyde, William, 1910, 125.
17. DeWitt Hyde, William, 1910, 127.
18. DeWitt Hyde, William, 1910, 135.
19. DeWitt Hyde, William, 1910, 153.

Chapter 16

Comparison of the two Theologies

It is quite amazing that even though they lived in New England and both were affiliated in one form or another with Harvard University, they lived at slightly different times. DeWitt Hyde was born in 1858, three years before Whitehead's birth. DeWitt Hyde died in 1917, seven years before Whitehead arrived at Harvard in 1924. DeWitt Hyde and Whitehead were both gifted intellectually, but DeWitt Hyde had none of the advantage in his early youth that Whitehead possessed. Fortunately for DeWitt Hyde, the sad early passage of his mother and father still ultimately led him to a home where they also valued education and this led him to a Harvard admission. Whitehead's father was a parson, and he guided both Alfred and his brother, Henry, educationally in terms of teaching, sharing, and encouraging knowledge and wisdom.

It is uncanny that Whitehead and DeWitt Hyde both held very similar views. They believed that any world with an external God led to fallacies in the proofs for the existence of God but also the external notion was inconsistent with a truly personal God. God is immanent and yet transcendent to the temporal world since he is both beyond time and also the essential element in the fabric of the world. Whitehead established this on a firm logical footing through a study of process, but DeWitt Hyde recognized the teleology present, and that the physical laws represented the Absolute Mind whereas the guide towards moral order represented the Absolute Will or what Whitehead called the lure. Whitehead, however, goes beyond DeWitt Hyde in that he saw the whole process as a movement toward aesthetic order. In terms of a personal God, both DeWitt Hyde and Whitehead, as seen in previous quotes, see him as intimately entwined with our personal world as both a comforter-healer as well as the very substrate of our spiritual existence.

Even though Whitehead views religion as fundamentally about the individual and his relation to the world he understands, as DeWitt Hyde shows, that social theology is the means for the individual to obtain God's lure or the Universal Will. Whitehead explains that: "Religion is force of belief cleansing the inward parts. For this reason the primary religious virtue is sincerity, a penetrating sincerity."[1]

For DeWitt Hyde, he views religion as a means of aiding the Universal Will by laying the groundwork for individual behavior, which leads to harmony for the individual and the society. Thus, as we saw in a previous chapter, he focuses on the fundamental factors that affect our character. How do we draw the cross between the self and others? The notions of sin, law, punishment, guilt, forgiveness, and the nature of prayer are examined. The truly religious person needs to examine and live these issues and see how they resolve in favor of a better self and a better world. The devil is in the details for DeWitt Hyde while Whitehead paints in broader abstract strokes.

On the question of evil in the world, we have already discussed Whitehead's position so now let us examine DeWitt Hyde's perspective. From the book, *The Gospel of Goodwill*, he states: "Accident, sickness, poverty, loneliness, unpopularity, failure, sin, bereavement, death—one or more of these evils confronts us most of the time: no one can escape them altogether."[2] He then goes on to talk about natural evils such as earthquakes and tornadoes and such forces that create them by following rigid physical laws. Neither we nor God in general can magically remove the forces and evils. He says: "Prayer which rests on and fosters that delusion is perverse; fatal to true worship and rational comfort."[3]

DeWitt Hyde understands the cross that evil brings but recognizes that by carrying out empathy, help and good will, independent of religious affiliations, when evil strikes, is part of our relationship with God. Through faith, charity, hope, and rationality man can possibly overcome evil and bring comfort to the sufferer. In the end, despite the problem of evil, it is treated similarly to Whitehead's approach, namely to place it in the very nature of the universe, for Whitehead in creativity and the eternal forms, but not in the nature of a non-temporal God.

DeWitt Hyde discusses societal issues in his books. For example, in *The Gospel of Goodwill*, he speaks about how, despite their immaculate dress and their silk hats, the leaders of some industries ignore the consequences of their actions because of the need for big profits. "This is why our railroads yearly injure one employee in twenty-six, and we look in vain for that promised 'day of the Lord' that will make a man more precious than fine gold."[4] For the next quote and for the above quote one has to remember how bad unrestrained capitalism was at the time when Teddy Roosevelt and the muckraker journalists helped change the world of the early 1900s:

"The rookery landlord and the jerry-builder, the adulterator and the maker and vendor of deleterious patent medicines, the quack doctor and charlatan 'healer', the purveyor of polluted water and infected milk, the man who fails to fence dangerous machinery and provide safety couplers for his cars, the owners of unsanitary tenements and fire-trap theaters, the men who overwork children, and employ women on conditions fatal to either health or character,-these murderers, numbered by hundreds, and whose victims are counted by tens of thousands, are the ones who do the wholesale human slaughter of today. There are a hundred times as many men guilty of murder through commercial complicity in the United States today as there were five hundred years ago, when the bow and arrow and the tomahawk were the weapons employed."[5]

Therefore, he had a progressive agenda; however, on other issues the progressive notions then seem reactionary today.

Societal issues at the time were discussed by Whitehead in Lucien Price's book, *Dialogues of Alfred North Whitehead*, which dealt with his weekly evening meetings with students and others. Whitehead was enamored with America. He loved the egalitarian nature of America and felt that the founding fathers were gifted and the creation of the Constitution was just right in terms of great generalities and fewer specifics. Boston was thriving and benefiting from the new emerging industries. He also expressed his belief that the role of a democracy is to relieve the burdens and miseries affecting the masses and yet preserve each individual's freedom as much as possible. He also believed that force should be used by the government only when clearly necessary. I believe his opinion was that governments overstepped their bounds, in forcing men to fight wars or punish individuals for using their freedom of expression.

He loved the students at Harvard who had great respect for him and the institution. He supported Franklin Delano Roosevelt and the New Deal. The year 1941 was a difficult year for him because his son, daughter-in-law, and grandson were in England and were subjected to the bombing raids. He always carefully followed all of the developing news in England.

Whitehead and DeWitt Hyde had similar views regarding fundamental abstract notions pertaining to their theologies. However, DeWitt Hyde was more interested in clarifying the gritty reality of how abstract religious thought could change an individual's ethical and moral behavior. Both men were committed to stringent logical reasoning as the basis for truth no matter where that led. They saw a world where God was actively guiding humans on their quest for achieving aesthetic harmony in their intertwined lives despite the world's inherent evils.

NOTES

1. Whitehead, Alfred North, *Religion*, 1926, 13.
2. DeWitt Hyde, William, *Social Theology*, 1917, 174.
3. DeWitt Hyde, William, *Social Theology*, 1917, 174.
4. DeWitt Hyde, William, *Gospel of Goodwill*, 1917, 86.
5. DeWitt Hyde, William, *Gospel of Goodwill*, 1917, 86.

Chapter 17

Science and Religion

Science is the study of our world which we now know is composed of matter and various forms of energy. Science is based on fundamental facts regarding the object or event of study. It stretches from inductive reasoning to abstract and universal laws regarding the nature of change and stability. Science starts with a series of questions followed by observation and facts. Newton observed the apple fall from the tree and desired to describe the nature of the force leading to its fall. These relationships were generalized with calculus and found to hold for other situations and became Newton's laws of motion.

Religion is more difficult to define but starts with existential questions that the earliest rational men and women asked. Why am I here? What value is my life? Why are there so many evils in my world? Is there a god with intelligence and power connected to our world? What will happen to me when my family and friends die? Why do people often hurt one another? The answers to these questions did not have the luxury of scientific experimentation and primitive religions often created anthropomorphic stories to explain them. American Indians believed that upon death, one went to the "Happy Hunting Ground" where game was plenty and life was good. Fear was a driving force in early religions and often required a need to pacify the god or gods. As religion became more rational, the gods were replaced with one God and the wrath of God was tempered by the love of God.

HOW DO YOU JUDGE TRUE SCIENCE
AND TRUE RELIGION?

Truth in science comes about by the realization that the old theory failed to be consistent with newer facts. Sometimes with great resistance new theories slowly topple old ones. For example, Boltzmann's theory of interpreting thermodynamics was met with great resistance for quite a while until more facts proved it overwhelmingly to be true.

Because of the giant scope of the topics, some theories involving climate change or the Big Bang cannot be tested experimentally a priori; however, massive amounts of interconnected data and known physical theories about our world and universe confirm their general truthfulness with considerable certainty. As seen in a previous chapter, some theories like Newtonian mechanics are true within a limited framework, as discovered later, when they attempted to apply them to very small particles like electrons or very large accelerating bodies where one needs either quantum mechanics, relativity, or both.

Assessing truth in religion is more difficult since the object to assess, namely deity, underlies the very core of the universe's existence. While most people have believed in the existence of God or gods, how do we know his existence makes logical sense? Atheists say we don't need deity to explain the universe. Whitehead, as we have seen, approached this question scientifically in that he tried to understand "process" or change inherent to our world in terms of fundamental postulates, and he could not make logical sense of our world's ever-changing nature, as we have shown, without invoking God. Order and harmony would be impossible without him.

While not a rigorous proof, it is consistent with all aspects of the material and spiritual world that we know.

BEYOND BELIEF IN GOD: CAN WE ASSESS WHETHER THE OVERALL IMPACT OF A GIVEN RELIGIOUS SYSTEM IS GOOD OR BAD FOR BOTH THE SOCIETY AND THE INDIVIDUAL?

Any religion that clings to the misguided notion that their beliefs are the ultimate unchanging truth would be a sign of a failed religion. Usually this is the case where dogma becomes overwhelming. For example, if you believe that my slightly different denomination will never see God, but only yours will, then that is a problem. Any religion that is static and does not relish new knowledge and bring new ideas into the religion is doomed by its rigidity. A constrictive religion that doesn't allow its members certain fundamental individual freedoms is limited. Any religion that believes that God chooses violence over persuasion as a usual tool of religion is not a viable religion. Any religion that does not attempt to recognize some potential value in every soul is a limited religion.

Thus, a religion must be just, humble, honest, give hope to the weary, and give charity to the needy. It must promulgate its religion by example. Why are these few fundamental principles for religion necessary? Because any God, worthy of worship, would have to lead people individually and collectively to a better place.

HOW HAS SCIENCE AFFECTED
RELIGION AND VICE VERSA?

When the earth-centered universe gave way to scientific advancement, Galileo remarked in an essay entitled *Letter to the Grand Dutchess Christina (1615)*: "It is surely harmful to souls to make it a heresy to believe what is proved."[1] The transformation demanded a newer view of the cosmos and should not have been viewed as heresy.

Another significant challenge to religion, especially for conservative Christians, came with Darwin's theory of evolution. Not being at the center of God's attention and having to evolve from other living creatures, with all of the associated struggles, seems, to these groups, inconsistent with God's plan. Yet, as discussed earlier, most religions now accept scientific evolution as a matter of fact, but they recognize that it is unacceptable to apply the simplistic concept of "survival of the fittest" to man in the sense of working against justice, harmony, and peace, since humans are evolving in a parallel spiritual plane, not definable in scientific terms.

Future potential adjustment by religion will probably involve scientific advances regarding the physical basis of consciousness and reasoning. Another area of challenge could be related to advances in robotics or the discovery of advanced life forms from other planets.

Science, on the other hand, often has a problem of overconfidence and overreach beyond science into areas that are not scientific. Some scientists see religion as unnecessary and believe science is the only truth. They have to come to grips with the fact that their worldview is itself based upon abstract notions reflective of a fundamental intelligence supporting our existence. No scientific proof exists for the nonexistence of God and while some can speculate about the existence of other universes and their probabilistic consequences, the reality is that invoking other universes just extends the unbelievable mystery of our existence.

IMPORTANCE OF SCIENCE AND RELIGION

The relative importance of science to society versus the importance of religion to society is complicated. Science has transformed our ability to live with more comfort and overall has resulted in a longer life span than previous centuries. Science has led to unprecedented forms of travel and communication. Science and technology are founded on rational approaches to understanding nature and transforming materials for our betterment. All this material progress has also resulted in our pollution of our atmosphere and climate change. Increased ease of communication has positively transformed our lives but has also made it possible for governments and fringe groups to exert authoritarian principles and to promulgate illogical conspiracy theories. Science has given us the enormous energy buried in the nucleus of atoms, which also unfortunately could lead to the annihilation of mankind. Science has become a god and a genie that grants amazing power but demands a society capable of moral integrity.

Worldwide religious organizations have, in the last two hundred years, diminished in size. Religion's value can come from its fundamental approach towards living your life, which bears on your ethical beliefs, love, views on war and peace, charity, hope, and death. It affects the very nature of a society but still currently lacks the universality of core beliefs, which transcend different religions. However, it has produced the Judeo-Christian justice system which is the main support for our modern social order. One can argue that democratic political systems are founded on the primacy of the individual and his individual worth, and this is also a fundamental tenant in the Judeo-Christian tradition. As mentioned before, not all religions progress society; some become stagnant and unwilling to allow fresh ideas into their frozen theology. Some "religions" as mentioned earlier are downright evil. Religion seeks answers to the big questions of life and death, whereas science seeks the unveiling of truths relegated to narrower domains where testing can allow for verification. Both seek answers to the riddles of the universe and hope that by finding them, people will benefit from their success.

Conflicts arise that are often politicized and this can distort both science and religion. Economic motives, as in the case of climate change, can interweave with certain religious notions and present a united front, which allows for the continued irrational emphasis on using fossil fuels, and consequently damages society in the long term. Combined with this is an anti-intellectual bias that distrusts the motives of "experts" whom they associate with a liberal, permissive society which overlooks certain perceived moral evils. Such conservatism is counter to the overall common good as it is really a radical departure from rational discourse and sometimes even embraces magical thinking.

Both religion and science have their moments of failed theories or beliefs. They move on different planes or spheres and both seek the truth yet religion's scope encompasses the spiritual aspects of the whole universe, our individual universe, and our individual souls.[2] Science's truths are generally restricted to certain specific objective aspects of the universe. Both approaches need to accept their limitations. In terms of religion, understanding God and the universe and ourselves is only a work in progress. Scientists need to understand that, while the mind of God has been partly found within beautiful theories such as Quantum Mechanics and Relativity, the nonphysical world is a different, complex reality, not fully amenable to mathematical formulations.

NOTES

1. Galilei, Gailileo, and Drake, Stillman, *Discoveries*, 1957.
2. Gould, Stephan Jay, *Rock of Ages*, 2011.

Chapter 18

Religion's Trajectory

A hundred years ago, Whitehead envisioned in the last paragraph of *Religion in the Making*, as shown in chapter ten, how significantly the world and its people would change.[1] In the past one-hundred years we saw the rise of unimaginable weapons and technology. The years have seen the advent of powerful antibiotics and other medications. The genetic code has been unraveled. A significant lengthening, until now with Covid-19, of life expectancy has occurred. The century saw a rise and fall of communism and fascism but now again democracy is in peril. Fantastic modes of visual communication with the advent of the internet have transformed our world. On the negative side, the horrors of the Second World War and the dropping of nuclear weapons in Japan have not cured us of violent transgressions. Education has progressed worldwide in this time interval. Women have made great strides, especially in western countries, in terms of education and employment.

Religion has changed in these one-hundred years. Christianity, as mentioned previously, is now practiced by a much smaller percentage of the world's population. More importantly, the attendance to formal services in general trends downward. Morality has often been redefined in egocentric terms rather than actual social justice terms. Whereas the reformation cleaved the bonds from Papal control, the last one hundred years have cleaved religion from its social moorings to a more personal, spiritual relationship with God. The risk with this shift is a potential decline in social and moral responsibility and the development of irrational religious notions, while the benefit is increased freedom from rigid dogma.

Changes over the years have been dramatic, and even recent singular events such as 9/11 or Covid-19 can transform the world and the world of religion. Will religion in the next one hundred years be further transformed into a personal spiritual belief system devoid of denominations or even a fixed religious group? To what extent will religious organizations change and adopt less rigid dogmas and boundaries? The answer to the latter question will partly determine the answer to the former question. It seems currently that religious organizations will have difficulty with changing their dogmas but even if they succeed, they need to broaden their appeal, and this appears unlikely to occur. This is also complicated by religious organizations tending to align with certain political groups, which then further narrows their appeal. Therefore, it seems that the move to a more personal religion will continue.

Religious and moral education needs to be revitalized; however, who is going to achieve this if the religious organizations continue to fail? Can religious education be unbiased? Whitehead's Process Theology is very general; however, in treating the consequent nature of God, he reflects active Christian ideas, whereas eastern religious notions tend to be more passive and more consistent with the primordial nature of God. The answer to the question about bias in teaching religion is that dogma must be taught as not fixed in stone, and that some fundamental concepts are common to all religions that respect all people's individual and collective worth. As to who can carry out such religious education, it may be that an intelligent and moral group arises out of the younger generation who go beyond formal religion and teach a more universal type of religion and morality.

Will people become more moral, less selfish, and socially responsible as time passes through this century? The average trend seems to be currently in the opposite direction; however, ultimately it will be a different view of religion, morality, and social responsibility that will supplant the current view. Major events and discoveries combined with improved worldwide education will reshape religious notions, but God's lure towards a more harmonious and aesthetic order will survive.

NOTE

1. Whitehead, Alfred North, *Religion*, 1926, 140.

Chapter 19

Miracles and Mortality

A miracle is difficult to define partly because of its extraordinary nature. Webster begins the definition as follows: "A miracle is an event not ascribable to human power or the laws of nature and consequently attributed to a supernatural, especially divine, agency." What we ascribe as the laws of nature can eventually be found to have exceptions, which often leads to a modification of the laws. Care must be taken in ascribing a true miracle based on this definition regarding the laws of nature and on encountering unusual events.

For example, the extraordinary powers seen with people known as idiot savants who can perform amazing feats such as memorizing a whole book or performing mental calculations seem humanly impossible, but they are not miracles. Another example would relate to the early moments of the Big Bang where all the known laws of physics break down and creation seems miraculous, yet it may eventually be explained by science.

In assessing whether a given event is miraculous or not, we take into account the veracity and weight of evidence of witnesses, how they reacted to the event and the strength of their convictions regarding it. One can use quantitative probability theory methods to evaluate the likelihood of a miracle occurring in comparison with the lack of evidence. A problem with using deductive reasoning alone is that the logical conclusion is binary, either true or false. For example, a historical argument put forward by Victorian logicians goes something like this:[1] (1) A miracle which is attested to by many who bore suffering and pain through their lives in support of its validity is consistent with a miracle. (2) Christian miracles are consistent with 1. (3) The Christian miracles are thus valid. There is some truth in that the first statement may be consistent with a miracle; however, it is not sufficient. For example, the apostles believed in the principles of Christianity that Christ taught, rather than just a belief in his performed miracles. His overall teachings, sacrifice, and belief in his kinship with the Divine may have been sufficient for their dedication without a belief that his actions were miraculous.

Deductive reasoning requires qualifications, and thus one can try to define certain criteria which if satisfied correspond to a miracle. For example, the following four criteria for a miracle suggested by Charles Leslie as presented in the online Stanford philosophy library:[1] (1) That the matters of fact be such, as that men's outward senses, their eyes and ears, may be judges of it. (2) That it be done publicly in the face of the world. (3) That not only public monuments be kept up in memory of it, but some outward actions to be performed. (4) That such monuments, and such actions or observances, be instituted, and do commence from the time that the matter of fact was done. The problems here are that each criterion is not sufficient, and the assumption that collectively they should be true is not necessary but also not sufficient. Visual impressions can be deceiving in that what is interpreted as an image of a sacred figure appearing on a wall just seems like a disordered stain to another. Also the criteria used may miss other important evidence.

Another approach is to list a set of explanatory facts such as: Jesus died on the cross. His followers saw him after his death. The followers became bold apostles for Christ. Paul is transformed from persecutor of Christ to follower after a miraculous event. All of these appear initially to be true statements; however, they fail to prove the resurrection since each statement is challengeable and thus has to have further clarification.

So we still have the probabilistic approach which weighs the mathematical odds via Bayesian analysis. One starts out with a starting probability of the miracle being true as zero, then as each piece of information from witnesses and their reactions is added, it either increases the odds in favor closer to 1 or can decrease towards zero. For example, one witness' statement might increase the odds to say to 0.5 and another drop it to 0.2. Someone could also add negative information that should be considered such as reasons for the nonexistence of miracles. For example, the philosopher, Spinoza, gave the following argument against all miracles: (1) The will of God is identical with the laws of nature. (2) A miracle is a violation of the laws of nature. (3) Necessarily, God's will is inviolable. Therefore: (4) Miracles cannot happen.

Clearly there is a problem with this argument. Point number 3 would mean that God would not allow for a very rare violation of the law in order to encourage goodness to flourish and still keep man's free will essentially intact. On the other hand, the order in the world is one of the arguments for God and a lack of order would lead to chaos. Another problem is trying to understand why God would allow a miracle to occur in one instance and not in another. Why part the Red Sea but not save the world from the Holocaust?

Others argue that miracles are so unlikely to occur that it is much more likely that the witnesses made an error or lied. So we can see the difficulty of any proof of a given miraculous claim and how general beliefs about God and the world influence opinion.

Now that we have explored this complexity, let us see how Whitehead and DeWitt Hyde viewed miracles. Whitehead's Process Theology is built on the idea that God is noncoercive. He does not force his will and interfere with our freedoms. It is based on reason, not revelation. In that sense a miracle would be a disruption from God's overall approach. However, we are somewhat coerced, even in Process Theology, in the sense that our physical laws are set and we have had no choice in that actuality. One could read the imaginative miracles in religious texts as giving men spiritual hopes since through God's graces mankind has the ability, with the hard work of learning, to create their own "miracles" which can overcome enemies, illnesses, and sin. On the other hand, Whitehead recognized the world's complexity of forms and spirits allows for extraordinary evils but at the same time accommodates extraordinary positive events. Thus, he always had an open mind to any new evidence that might clarify the miraculous event.

Furthermore, quantum mechanics and statistical mechanics show us that low probability events, that would not happen in classical mechanics, are fundamental to their structure and do occur. As an example, random mutations of DNA can occur because of quantum tunneling, which is classically analogous to the impossible or miraculous chance that a house cat could jump over a twenty-foot wall.

In addition, the miraculous is subjective in the sense that if, for example, I believe that this special bath I take is curative, my body, through my mind's belief, causes epigenetic changes which in turn releases various chemicals. These in turn relieve stress, increase blood flow, lower blood pressure and heart rate which assist me in healing. Just positive thoughts alone can be transformative as Francis Hodgson Burnett stated in the book, The Secret Garden: "One of the new things people began to find out in the last century was that thoughts—just mere thoughts—are as powerful as electric batteries. . . ."[2]

DeWitt Hyde viewed the miraculous as not the foundation of Christian thought but rather the message of love, caring, and respect present in Christ's message. According to DeWitt Hyde from his book, *Social Theology*:

"The argument for the divinity of Christ from prophecy and miracles is absolutely destitute of cogency for the representative modern mind. Miracles are at best merely the scaffolding or decoration, not the foundation and substance of Christian faith. Ten times the miracles ascribed to Jesus, supported by ten times the evidence, would not be sufficient to convince us that Nero was the Son of God."[3]

DeWitt Hyde, as mentioned before, points out that the natural laws are what they are and we usually don't look for law-violating miracles to heal us. "When . . . I call in a physician I do not ask him to change that law in my behalf. I ask him to bring to bear other laws. I ask him to introduce into the problem the action of certain chemicals upon the infected tissues . . . The physician brought not less law, but more."[4] DeWitt Hyde implores us to be fighters against evil in this world as in the *Sermon on the Mount*. He expressed the bigger picture of our miraculous special existence in God's presence. The physical laws exist and the miraculous is not in their direct negation but rather demands our ingenuity to bypass the issue through another physical or spiritual approach. The miracle Christ taught was that deep down within us is the possibility that our thoughts and actions can save our individual souls and collectively our society.

Thus, the role of miracles in theology should be viewed as a metaphor for God's lure towards goodness and healing yet at the same time it should be viewed as a manifestation of God's extraordinary existence that he shares with us. C.S. Lewis and G. K. Chesterton both recognized that our spiritual existence is miraculous in itself. For Christians, the Resurrection of Christ is a marker for all of our afterlives shared with him and is a miracle fundamental to the faith. Belief in an afterlife; however, predates Christianity and we examine mortality and the afterlife next.

MORTALITY AND THE AFTERLIFE

Many tales have been told of insight into the world beyond our existence as people approached death only to be brought back from the brink. Why should mankind have generally and persistently believed in some form of afterlife? One reason may be the dichotomy that was felt between mind or spirit and the physical body. Clearly, even without the knowledge of science, early humans recognized that the mind or spirit was gone with the death of the body. However, in the memory of survivors they were still present and as they remembered their teachings and feelings. In the early twentieth century, the attending of séances was popular. Someone within the group would attempt to communicate with a dead friend or relative.

Plato in *The Republic* gives the myth of the Soldier Er who died and came back to tell of what he saw in the afterlife:

" . . . he returned to life and told them what he had seen in the other world. He said that when his soul left the body he went on a journey with a great company, and that they came to a mysterious place at which there were two openings in the earth; they were near together, and over against them were two other openings in the heaven above.

In the intermediate space there were judges seated, who commanded the just, after they had given judgment on them and had bound their sentences in front of them, to ascend by the heavenly way on the right hand; and in like manner the unjust were bidden by them to descend by the lower way on the left hand; these also bore the symbols of their deeds, but fastened on their backs."[5]

Religious groups from most faiths allude to an afterlife. For example, in the Old Testament:

Dan 12:1–3: "At that time Michael, the great prince who protects your people, will arise. There will be a time of distress such as has not happened from the beginning of nations until then. But at that time your people—everyone whose name is found written in the book—will be delivered. Multitudes who sleep in the dust of the earth will awake: some to everlasting life, others to shame and everlasting contempt. Those who are wise will shine like the brightness of the heavens, and those who lead many to righteousness, like the stars forever and ever."

Muslims believe in the continued existence of the soul and a transformed physical existence after death. They also believe there will be a day of judgment when all humans will be divided between good and evil.

Buddhism teaches that after death one is either reborn into another body (reincarnated), or one will achieve the ultimate nirvana (enlightenment). Christianity believes in the resurrection of the body and a heavenly afterlife with Christ. For example, in the parable of the rich man and Lazarus, Christ shows that the injustices of this world need to be rectified in the afterlife in accordance with a just God. The joy of eternal life with Christ is contrasted by the horrors of damnation. If you rise to the level of a just and honorable human life, then you will find joy with a loving God in the breadth of another existence beyond time.

However, there is no way we can prove the existence of an afterlife in any traditional scientific sense since science needs reproducible observations and any observations are performed by an observer while alive. Some people have experienced near-death experiences that on "return" claim information, but these observations are not easily reproducible and could be related to dreamlike states. The closest we have come to objective observations were the experiences and writings of the apostles.

Let us now take a look at what Whitehead and DeWitt Hyde said about an afterlife. DeWitt Hyde addressed the issue briefly in *Outlines of Social Theology* and said it was not scientifically provable but the lack of immortality would be: "Inconsistent with all that we know of the wisdom and love of God . . . inconsistent with the deepest intuitions and hopes of the human heart."[6] And also:

"Annihilation of those who have wrought out their sonship to God and their membership in his kingdom through the hard conflicts of earth and time, and the creation of others to take their places, certainly does not seem either an economical, or a just, or a kind mode of procedure. It is inconsistent with the fatherhood of God. It robs the life of man of its deepest and widest significance."[7]

Whitehead was amused about the traditional view of heaven. In one of his weekly meetings at his home with fellow students and faculty as documented in Lucien Price's *Dialogues of Alfred North Whitehead*, he wondered about how the traditional views of heaven have no challenges or problems to solve.[8] On the other hand, as seen in his quote at the end of our chapter fourteen, Whitehead strongly believes that God incorporates each parcel of experience within himself and without this objective immortality, our lives would be meaningless. He implies, as above, that how our immortality plays out beyond this world is probably much more complex than traditional notions of heaven or hell. So Whitehead, in this regard, appears to believe in the miraculous.

NOTES

1. Stanford Encyclopedia of Philosophy, *Miracles*, 2019.
2. Burnett, Francis Hodgson, *Secret Garden*, 1911.
3. DeWitt Hyde, William, *Social Theology*, 1910, 70.
4. DeWitt Hyde, William, 1910, 120.
5. Plato, 2007, *The Republic*, 10–614.
6. DeWitt Hyde, William, 1910, 255.
7. DeWitt Hyde, William, 1910, 256.
8. Price, Lucien, *Dialogues*, 1954.

Chapter 20

Wisdom

Wisdom hovers over and above human knowledge, for it encompasses both abstract notions and the practicality of achieving human goals. To what extent does what we have discussed in this book have the potential to aid in our personal and collective wisdom? However, what do we mean by wisdom?

A wise person has knowledge of the most valuable goals for his life, and has recognition of how feasible, difficult, dangerous, and costly the path towards these goals might be. As in Matthew 10:16: "Behold, I send you forth as sheep in the midst of wolves: be ye therefore wise as serpents, and harmless as doves." You need to understand the forces against you and still understand what was said in James 1:19, 20: "Wherefore, my beloved brethren, let every man be swift to hear, slow to speak, slow to wrath: For the wrath of man worketh not the righteousness of God."

A person needs the ability to judge people and events correctly and to follow the best course of action based hopefully on knowledge and experience obtained during one's lifetime. The ability to see beneath the surface of things is critical. So far we haven't said anything about the nature of the goals one seeks. A person who only cares about money might have an evil goal which creates wealth for him by cheating, conning, and damaging other people. Can this man be considered wise? Aristotle felt it was impossible to be wise if one is not ethical overall.[1] He believed that only by having just ways of desiring could one achieve man's true nature and find happiness in the long run. The selfish man who burdens others for his own gratification creates pain and suffering in the community and *eventually* the collective wisdom of the community will make their judgment on this man.

Morality is essential for true wisdom and while one could dissociate morality and wisdom, a problem arises. Goals must be consistent with personal benefits and helping the community also but at least, not intentionally hurting the community. Thus, a wise person seeks truth in his beliefs and direction. Wisdom requires being "street wise" but also demands rising above the current personal situation to a more objective consideration.

Socrates believed that if a man thought he was wise, it was more likely that he was not. He believed that the gods alone had true wisdom and that the best of our wisdom was significantly limited. Our knowledge, which allows us to predict events, is still limited especially in complex systems such as global finance, earthquake prediction or in relation to our lives. Also a wise man with tremendous knowledge and skill can be completely pushed off track by random events. As above, if a man says he is wise, he most probably is not, whereas if a man believes he is not wise, he may very well be correct.

Wisdom, which is partly related to professing knowledge, demands adherence to truth. Today, people seem more gullible than centuries ago, which may be an effect of mass media and the internet. Many people need to learn to test conspiracy theories by understanding probabilities or likelihood that an explanation is plausible and then ranking it against other explanations. At the same time, they can't let the personal or political consequences of believing in a theory decide what is true. Conspiracy theories that attempt to explain an assassination can make some sense because if one assumes one lone person was responsible, then, if the facts lead you to evidence of other participants, it is reasonable to assume a conspiracy exists. However, some conspiracies are incredibly unlikely from the start. For example, the idea that President Obama caused Hurricane Sandy in order to get reelected borders on the ridiculous. The believer proposed that a special ultrasound system from the government was used to create the hurricane. Clearly, political conspiracy theories have the advantage of hurting a candidate. No such ultrasound system exists and if it did someone would have leaked it. An obviously extremely likely alternative to this would be that hurricanes happen at that time of year and some are powerful. The media needs to nip these crazy theories in the bud. Elvis is still alive, the moon landing was a hoax, alien genes, Pizzagate, and "Deep State" represents other examples. We have entered a post-truth era and if we don't get back to a truth era, the lack of truthfulness may lead to our planet's demise.

Both Whitehead and DeWitt Hyde were committed to finding the truth about man and his universe. While one was the son of a minister and the other was an ordained minister, both were educators who believed that rationality could help unlock the secrets of the spiritual world. That commitment meant following wherever the factual realities led them. Their religious background, however, helped them to appreciate the long history of religious belief.

There is a notion called Solomon's Paradox, which says that Solomon was clearly a wise man but that most of his wisdom was in relation to making decisions for others instead of for him. Without commenting on Solomon's life, clearly the phenomenon does exist. While wise for others, how wise were Whitehead and DeWitt Hyde in their personal lives? Whitehead seemed to heed the advice he gave to the world. As a theorist he stayed mostly in the university ivory tower, yet his reach stretched to the far corners of the universe of man and the fundamental meaning of our existence. While he and his family suffered from the death of his pilot son in World War One, he and his wife worked hard to overcome it and in his theories, he elaborated how purpose and meaning were possible even in a tragically flawed universe. While our knowledge about his personal life is limited, he seemed capable of making valuable choices and really caring about others.

DeWitt Hyde saw social theology as his mission and he achieved this mission with his writing, teaching, and leadership at Bowdoin College. In many ways, he gave more than he received, for he understood that was the price for his Christian leadership. He believed that the Christian way of life demands sacrifice. He clearly found a path and worked to succeed. His mind was brilliant, but he never achieved the full intellectual flourishing of which he was capable because his leadership at the school was very demanding. He was happy in his life and true to reason, family, and society. He was a bearer of wisdom.

How do the fundamental religious notions reflected in the seven riddles help us to achieve wisdom? Again, knowledge only takes you so far, and then you need to have reasonable goals and just actions to accomplish them. The fundamental religious notions help to shape our goals from a more global perspective. These notions clarify our place in the world and illuminate our potential achievements during the time of our existence. The interconnectedness of everything should be seen as a need to respect truth, beauty, and justice. The order in the world and the evidence for an intelligent deity who guides us on the path to a better place and who in his quest for truth and beauty cares for each and every soul, despite our limited nature and the existence of evil in the world, gives us hope and perspective regarding our daily problems and emotions. Understanding his ethics can help drive our wills to aid in his goals, as well as our goals. His understanding of suffering and his forgiveness for the truly repentant assists us with showing similar compassion to others. He mollifies our emotional rages, not from the perspective of acceptance, but rather from the more global value achieved by a fuller perspective.

The fact that our work, suffering, love, and caring have meaning as each actual occasion is incorporated into God's nature means that life is also valuable to future times and to ourselves. In our times of despair, these notions can sometimes carry us through the difficulties we face and the feelings of being forsaken. Wisdom demands an understanding of human limitations and the ability to forgive others and forgive ourselves. Wisdom demands an appreciation of each moment of peace and tranquility and simple joy allotted to us.

NOTE

1. Gellera, Gioanni, *Ethics*, 2017.

Bibliography

Bergson, Henri. *Matter and Memory*. United States: Dover Publications, 2012.

Burnett, Charles Theodore. *Hyde of Bowdoin A Biography of William De Witt Hyde*. Houghton Mifflin, 1931.

Burnett, Francis Hodgson. *The Secret Garden*. Penguin Classic, 1911.

Chang, Kenneth. *Japan's Journey to an Asteroid Ends with a Hunt in Australia's Outback. New York Times*, December 5, 2020, updated January 7, 2021.

Chesterton, Gilbert K. *Heretics*. John Lane Company, London, 1909.

DeWitt Hyde, William. *The Five Great Philosophies of Life*. The Macmillan Company, 1924.

DeWitt Hyde, William. *The Gospel of Goodwill*. The Macmillan Company, 1917.

DeWitt Hyde, William. *Outlines of Social Theology*. The Macmillan Company, 1910.

DeWitt Hyde, William. *Practical Ethics*. Henry Holt & Co., 1892.

DeWitt Hyde, William. *Practical Idealism*. The Macmillan Company, 1899.

Finkelstein, Gabriel. *Emil du Bois-Reymond: Neuroscience, Self, and Society in Nineteenth Century Germany*. The MIT Press, 2013.

Floyd, Stacey M., et al. *Liberation Theologies in the United States*. NYU Press, 2010.

Galilei, Galileo, and Drake, Stillman. *Discoveries and Opinions of Galileo*. Doubleday, 1957.

Galloway, George. *The Philosophy of Religion*. Charles Scribner's Sons, 1920.

Gamow, George. *One Two Three Infinity*. Dover Publications, 2012.

Gamow, George. *Thirty Years that Shook Physics–The Story of Quantum Theory*. Dover Publications, 2012.

Gellera, Gioanni. *An Analysis of Aristotle's Nicomachean Ethics*. United Kingdom: Macat Library, 2017.

Gould, Stephan Jay. Rock *of Ages–Science and Religion in the Fullness of Life*. United States, Random House Publishing, 2011.

Griffin, David R. *Reenchantment without Supernaturalism: A Process Philosophy of Religion*. Cornell University Press, 2001.

Haeckel, Ernst. *The Riddle of The Universe At The Close Of The Nineteenth Century.* Harper Brothers, 1905.

Harris, Roy. Ed. *Origin of Language.* United Kingdom, Bloomsbury Academic, 1996.

Hosinski, Thomas E. *Stubborn Fact and Creative Advance: An Introduction to the Metaphysics of Alfred North Whitehead.* United States: Rowman & Littlefield Publishers, 1993.

Johnson, A.H. Ed. *The Interpretation of Science.* Indianapolis: Bobbs-Merrill, 1961.

Kaku, Michio. *The Future of Humanity: Terraforming Mars, Interstellar Travel, Immortality, and Our Destiny Beyond Earth.* Doubleday, 2018.

Legendre, Matthieu, et al. *Thirty-thousand-year-old distant relative of giant icosahedral DNA viruses with pandoravirus morphology.* PNAS, 111(11) 4274–4279, March 18, 2014.

Lewis, C.S. *The Screwtape Letters.* HarperCollins, 2001.

Lowe, Victor. *Alfred North Whitehead: The Man and His Work.* Johns Hopkins University Press, 2020.

Mastin, L. Hydrothermal Vents, https://www.physicsoftheuniverse.com/topics_life_terrestrial.html, 2009.

McClure, Max. *Stanford Report Mycoplasma Computer Model.* https://biox.stanford.edu/highlight/stanfort-researchers-produce-first-complete-computer-model-organism, 2012.

McGrayne, Sharon Bertsch. *The Theory That Would Not Die.* Yale University Press, 2011.

McPherson, Jeffrey A. *Creativity in the Metaphysics of Alfred North Whitehead.* Thesis. McMaster University, 1996.

Muller, Johannes. *Elements of Physiology.* London Taylor & Walton, Cambridge University Library, 1838.

Nagel, Thomas. *Mind & Cosmos: Why the Materialist Neo-Darwinian Conception of Nature is Almost Certainly False.* Oxford University Press, 2012.

NASA. *COBE,* https://science.nasa.gov/missions/cobe, 2016.

O'Connor, J.J and Robertson, E.F. *Paul du Bois-Reymond (1831–1889) Biography.* https//mathshistory.standrews.ac.uk/Biographies/Du_Bois-Reymond/, updated 2005.

Penrose, Roger. *Shadows of the Mind A Search for the Missing Science of Consciousness.* Oxford University Press, 1996.

Pink, Thomas. *Free Will: A Very Short Introduction:* United Kingdom: Oxford Paperbacks, 2004.

Plato. *The Republic.* Penguin Classics, 2007.

Pomeroy, Ross. *Why Georges Lematre should be as famous as Einstein.* https://www.realscience.com/blog/2017/03/07/, 2017.

Price, Lucien. *Dialogues of Alfred North Whitehead.* Little, Brown, 1954.

Reymond, Estelle. *Two Great Scientists of the Nineteenth Century: Correspondence of Emil Du Bois-Reymond and Carl Ludwig.* The Johns Hopkins University Press, 1982.

Stanford Encyclopedia of Philosophy. *Miracles.* www.plato.stanford.edu/miracles, 2019.

Swinburne, Richard. *The Coherence of Theism*. Oxford University Press, 2016.

Teilhard de Chardin, Pierre. *The Phenomenon of Man*. Lulu.com, 2018.

Whitehead, Alfred North. *Aims of Education*. Simon & Schuster, 1929.

Whitehead, Alfred North. *Process and Reality* (Gifford Lectures, 1927–1928): University Press, 1929.

Whitehead, Alfred North. *Religion in the Making* (Lowell Lectures, 1926). United Kingdom: Macmillan, 1926.

Whitehead, Alfred North. *Science and the Modern World*. Cambridge University Press, 1929.

Wilder, Thornton. *The Bridge of San Luis Rey*. HighBridge Company, 2004.

Index

About the Author

Alexander Mazziotti MD, PhD, holds both a medical degree from Rutgers University (CMDNJ) and a PhD in chemical physics from Penn State University. He completed a postdoctoral position at Johns Hopkins University and served as assistant professor of chemistry at Barnard College, Columbia University. Dr. Mazziotti's publications cover numerous fields including quantum chemistry, quantum physics, physiology, cardiology, endocrinology, and gastroenterology. His practice of internal medicine and cardiology is located in Hawthorne, New Jersey.